How to live in a dangerous world

How to live in a dangerous world

Biblical pictures of modern perils

Roger Ellsworth

 EVANGELICAL PRESS

EVANGELICAL PRESS
Grange Close, Faverdale North Industrial Estate, Darlington,
Co. Durham, DL3 0PH, England

First published 1998

British Library Cataloguing in Publication Data available

ISBN 0 85234 416 3

Printed and bound in Great Britain by Creative Print and Design
Wales, Ebbw Vale

These chapters are dedicated to one of the lights of life, my daughter-in-law, Sarah.

Contents

Foreword

Contemporary Christianity is often crippled by the pervasive suspicion that things are worse now than they have ever been. This theory usually amounts to an excuse for moral failure and the belief that the Scriptures themselves are no longer relevant or sufficient for a believer to escape the perils of modern life. After all, one might reason, how can the Bible really help, when Christians today have it so much worse than even Jesus did? One song often sung in churches goes so far as to express this sense of hopelessness in the words: 'Lord Jesus, you know, if you're looking below, that it's worse now than then.'

In *How to Live in a Dangerous World*, Roger Ellsworth boldly asserts that the Word of God is as relevant as tomorrow's newspaper, that it *is* sufficient for our needs because humanity today is no more or less sinful than it has been since the Fall and God's solutions are still available. Though there may be more creative expressions of sin, or more opportunities to indulge in it, it is still true that 'There is no temptation that has taken you but such as is common to man.' Whether we face problems that affect the conscience of a nation, the life of a church, or the destiny of a soul, they are perils of which we are warned in Holy Scripture. Even more importantly, they are dangers which we can conquer, if not altogether avoid, if only we will follow the admonition God has left us in his Word.

No book could be more appropriate, nor more needed, for the twenty-first century than this one. Fortune 500 executives can fight God with no less abandon than the Philistines. Those who have relegated the Bible to a merely human book are no less in danger than Amaziah, who attempted to give a supernatural message a naturalistic explanation. Furthermore, our whole culture thinks God lucky to get whatever worship we may choose to throw his way, just as did Esau. Mr Ellsworth reminds us that the pitfalls and hazards we face are not really different at all.

Yet the greatest message of *How to Live in a Dangerous World* is the irrepressible hope that it offers. Along with the well-marked road-map that warns us of the hidden dangers, Roger Ellsworth expertly identifies the places where we may find life, overcome perils and obtain salvation. He carefully and compassionately mines the gems of the biblical text and lays their wealth before the reader, inviting us to help ourselves to their value.

Though this book is appropriate for every stage and every expression of the Christian life, it is also an evangelistic tool that can be given to those who face the greatest peril of all, rejection of God's gracious provision in Christ. An excellent tool for home Bible study, private devotion, classroom teaching and especially for preaching, this work is suited for anyone who has a desire to overcome the subtle pressures and problems that have plagued mankind for millennia and will continue into the next millennium.

I am overjoyed to recommend this book in the hope that it will bless and encourage others as it has me. Roger Ellsworth has once again pointed us to the sacred text and to its practical application to our lives. And for that I am most grateful.

Hershael W. York
Associate Professor of Preaching
Southern Baptist Theological Seminary

Preface

Everyone understands what it is to be in peril. It means we are exposed to some sort of danger, to something that has the potential for doing us great harm. And everyone understands that risks and dangers are a constant and ongoing part of life. There is no such thing as risk-free living. Our health is constantly put at risk by various diseases. Our possessions and even our very lives are in danger from criminals. Our finances are under threat from spiralling costs and unexpected catastrophes. Our marriages are in peril through misunderstanding, bickering and even divorce.

There is no way for us to get away from the risks and dangers of daily life. We are constantly reminded of them each and every day. When we turn on the television, or pick up the newspaper, we are confronted with dangers threatening the economy, the environment, the educational system, and so on.

Yes, we all understand what perils, or dangers, are and that they are a constant part of life. What we often do not understand is how subtle they can be. Not all are open and obvious. In fact, we can go so far as to say that we carry some of the most dangerous perils of all in our own minds. Yes, beliefs can be very dangerous indeed! The risks that we tend to be most concerned about are able to harm us only in this life, but mistaken beliefs can bring incalculable harm to us in the life to come.

The Bible is full of instruction on this matter of dangerous views. It is a veritable handbook on men and women and their mistaken notions, and where those notions led them. Sometimes it lays before us the dangerous views held by unbelievers, while at other times it shows us believers holding perilous notions. In each case, its purpose is to warn us away from these same dangers and, in so doing, to lead us into the happiness of knowing God and obeying his commands.

Beliefs and values are not matters of indifference. One is not as good as another. Our beliefs and values affect our behaviour, and our behaviour invites God's blessing or his judgement. So my purpose in these chapters is to isolate some of the major beliefs and values of our day, identify people in the Bible who held to them, and see where those beliefs and values led them. In doing so, we shall have a clear indication of where they are likely to lead those who hold them today.

Roger Ellsworth

Section I
Pictures of rejection

What is the most critical issue of our day? There is no shortage of answers. Education, the environment, crime, drug addiction, abortion and the cloning of human beings are all put forward as the answer.

Important as these matters are, they all pale in comparison with the issue set before us in the Word of God — the forgiveness of our sins through the salvation provided by God's Son, Jesus Christ. This matter far surpasses and outweighs all the others because they are concerned only with this temporal realm. Long after all these issues have ceased to be issues, each and every human being will be either in eternal bliss in heaven or eternal misery and woe in hell.

Does this seem to be overstating the case? The Lord Jesus himself consistently emphasized the priority of eternal salvation. He once asked, 'For what profit is it to a man if he gains the whole world, and loses his own soul? Or what will a man give in exchange for his soul?' (Matt. 16:26). On another occasion he said, 'And I say to you, my friends, do not be afraid of those who kill the body, and after that have no more that they can do. But I will show you whom you should fear: Fear him who, after he has killed, has power to cast into hell; yes, I say to you, fear him!' (Luke 12:4-5).

On yet another occasion, Jesus turned the attention of his hearers away from those who had perished in a temporal calamity, when a tower collapsed killing eighteen people, to the far worse calamity that would befall them if they refused to repent (Luke 13:4-5).

Then again, as he journeyed to Jerusalem he urged those around him not to assume that their eternal destiny would work out well without their paying any heed to the matter. Instead he told them to 'strive' to enter through the narrow gate that would eventually lead them to eternal life (Matt. 7:13-14; Luke 13:24).

To his hearers in Capernaum, the Lord Jesus made a clear statement on this question of priorities: 'Do not labour for the food which perishes, but for the food which endures to everlasting life, which the Son of Man will give you, because God the Father has set his seal on him' (John 6:27).

The examples quoted constitute only a meagre sampling of what Jesus had to say about the importance of eternal life. He was unrelenting at this point. There were all kinds of wrongs to be righted in society while Jesus was engaged in his public ministry. All sorts of beneficial programmes and organizations could have been started. But without denigrating the legitimacy of these things, Jesus consistently focused his attention on the supreme issue. He refused time after time to be swept along by the popular tide into a political kingship so that he could remain on course. And his course, assigned to him by his Father before the world began, was to provide forgiveness of sins and eternal life for all who would repent of their sins and believe in him.

The Lord Jesus said he had come 'to seek and to save' that which was lost (Luke 19:10). He said he had come to lay down his life as a 'ransom' for many (Mark 10:45). Jesus came to this earth with that ransom clearly in view. That ransom was to be provided on a Roman cross. There he would become a substitute for sinners and receive in his own person the just penalty of God's eternal wrath against them. God only demanded that this penalty be paid once and, if Jesus paid it on the cross, there would then be no penalty left for the believing sinner.

Jesus refused to be deterred or dissuaded from that cross. He pursued a straight and unwavering course towards it until he uttered from it the triumphant cry: 'It is finished!' (John 19:30). Because Jesus completely and perfectly finished the work of salvation, the happy invitation goes out to all to come and avail themselves of that finished work (Rev. 22:17).

We might expect that such wonderful news would be happily received by overwhelming numbers, but this is not the case. Even though this salvation is gloriously available, many turn away from it. They spurn their hope for eternal life by travelling the broad road that leads to eternal destruction (Matt. 7:13). Why do they do it? Why do they wage war on their own eternal well-being and refuse God's salvation? The Scripture's explanation is that they are blinded by Satan (2 Cor. 4:4). But Satan, that master deceiver, does not fish with only one hook. There is no end to his stratagems and devices. He blinds men and women to the glory of the gospel by ensnaring them in various pitfalls and temptations.

In the chapters that follow, we shall look at some of the perils to which men and women are exposed. They are not new. Satan has skilfully and successfully used them from the beginning of time until this present hour.

I should point out that there is some rather obvious overlapping in some of the areas we shall look at. By associating one individual with a particular peril or temptation, I do not mean to suggest that he was at risk from that one danger to the exclusion of all others. My purpose in associating each individual with one aspect of life in a dangerous world is to make that particular peril stand out in bold relief so that all who read these lines can see the danger and be warned by this person's example against falling into the same snare of the devil.

1.
Cain: a warning against self-centred living

Genesis 4:1-8

Self-centredness has become one of the most prominent features of our day. It used to be frowned on, but now it is regarded in many quarters as an essential part of wholesome and happy living.

Another word for self-centredness is 'narcissism', which is derived from the story of Narcissus, a young Greek athlete who was so preoccupied with himself that he was constantly gazing into a pond to see his reflection. This self-centredness, or narcissism, has been noted by both religious and secular leaders as a feature of contemporary society. A few years ago Harper's magazine published *The New Narcissism*. A *New Yorker* article by Tom Wolfe dubbed the decade of the seventies 'The Me Decade', and Christopher Lasch wrote a best seller in 1979 entitled *The Culture of Narcissism*.[1]

Self-centredness has always been with us. It began when Adam and Eve disobeyed God's command not to eat of the tree of knowledge of good and evil (Gen. 2:16-17). But while it began with them, it certainly did not end with them, but reached dreadful proportions in their son Cain.

If we are to see Cain's self-centredness, we must first understand that man was designed and constituted to have another centre. Man is not just a mere cosmic accident, or the sophisticated result of billions of years of evolution. He was made by

God and for God. Both the 'by' and the 'for' are essential. God is the one who made man, and he made man for the dual purpose of enjoying and glorifying God.

Everything went well for a time. Cain's parents Adam and Eve lived quite happily for some time in the Garden of Eden with God as the centre of their lives. Then one fateful day they disobeyed God's command and ate of the tree he had forbidden them (Gen. 3:1-7).

The essence of Adam and Eve's action was to remove God from the centre of their lives and to put themselves there. Sin is essentially the creature seeking to usurp the place of the Creator. As many have noted, the essence of sin is that it has an 'I' in the middle of it.

God would have been justified at that point if he had just wiped Adam and Eve off his earth, but he did something remarkably gracious and kind. He showed them the way in which the sin they had committed could be dealt with, and he could again be the centre of their lives. Their sin made them worthy of death, but God accepted the death of animals instead. He killed animals and made tunics of skin for Adam and Eve (Gen. 3:21). Adam and Eve learned, then, that the only way guilty sinners can approach a holy God is through the shedding of the blood of a substitute.

The manifestation of self-centredness

With all that in place, we are in a position to look at Cain and Abel and their offerings.

A casual reading of this account may cause us to wonder what all the fuss was about. It all sounds so innocent. Abel brought his offering to the Lord and Cain brought his. Why would God receive Abel's and reject Cain's? The answer is that when Cain brought his offering he was in fact putting himself in the centre. Yes, Adam and Eve had done the same thing when they sinned, but Cain's self-centredness was far more radical than that of his parents. When Adam and Eve were confronted with what they had done they sincerely repented and took advantage of the way God offered to deal with their sin. Cain, on the other hand, not only came to God in his self-centredness but stubbornly refused to back away from it.

Was all of this involved in the actions of Cain and Abel in bringing their offerings to the Lord? When Cain and Abel came along we can be sure that Adam and Eve carefully instructed them in this matter and carefully watched their sons to see how they responded to this teaching. S. G. DeGraaf writes, 'Believing parents are very perceptive. Adam and Eve could not help noticing that Abel believed the promise and gave his heart and life to the Lord in a simple way. But it did not escape their attention either that Cain wanted to live for himself. Deep in his heart Cain despised the Lord's promise and felt no need of deliverance. He was sure he could make it on his own.'[2]

When the day came for Cain and Abel to offer their own sacrifices to the Lord, what was in the heart of these two men came to the forefront. Abel submitted to the way God had revealed and came to him on the basis of the shed blood of an innocent substitute, but Cain despised this teaching and offered a bloodless sacrifice. Perhaps as he came to make his offering, Cain was saying to himself, 'I don't need to come God's way; my own way is good enough.'

We do not know the manner in which he did so, but in some way God indicated that he had accepted Abel's sacrifice and rejected Cain's. Some think he consumed Abel's sacrifice with fire while Cain's was left unburned. Others think God simply spoke from heaven.

Now we come to the point where Cain was given the opportunity to renounce his self-centred approach and to do things God's way. At this point, the Lord definitely did speak to Cain from heaven: 'If you do well, will you not be accepted?' (Gen. 4:7). Essentially, God was telling Cain to go back and bring the proper offering and all would be well.

God still has a way clearly marked out for salvation, and that way is the same now as it was in the Garden of Eden. No, we do not have to come to God with animal sacrifices because Jesus Christ came and shed his blood on the cross as the perfect substitute for sinners. But we have to come to God on the basis of that shed blood. We have to recognize that we have no merits of our own and trust completely in Jesus' death for our salvation.

But this is an age of self-centredness, or humanism. Humanism affirms that man himself is sufficient in all areas, that he does not need absolutes from God but can create his own absolutes apart from divine revelation. Many today join Cain in saying, 'I've got my own ideas about religion. I don't need to come God's way.' Those who do so would do well to thoroughly contemplate yet another aspect of the story of Cain — that is, where his actions led.

The results of self-centredness

The anger of Cain

First, he was extremely angry about God's rejection of his sacrifice. God's way seemed too narrow and demanding for him. Do we not see the very same anger today? Tell people that Jesus Christ and his blood sacrifice are the only way to get to heaven, and they become extremely angry and accuse us of being bigoted, narrow and rigid.

The murder of Abel

Secondly, Cain took his anger out on his brother Abel. No doubt Cain would have liked to kill God if he could, but since that was impossible he did the next best thing and killed one who loved God.

Even though thousands of years have come and gone, the humanistic mind has not changed in its make-up. It is still hostile to God and his way. And because it is powerless to touch God himself, it, like Cain, takes its anger out on the people of God. It is no accident that as humanism increases in modern Western society so does hostility towards biblical Christianity. The two always go together. There is a great irony here. Those who claim to be humanists pride themselves on being open-minded and tolerant, but they have very little tolerance for biblical Christianity.

The judgement of God

A third result of Cain's self-centred humanism was the judgement of God. His stubborn refusal to submit to God and his anger against God caused him to be driven into exile (Gen. 4:11-15) and to live in fear as a fugitive. What a dreadful price Cain had to pay for refusing to put God at the centre of his life! And, make no mistake about it, self-centred living still exacts a fearful toll from all who practise it. Those who refuse to come to God are driven away from his presence just as Cain was. The Bible makes it clear that the ultimate price of humanism is separation from God for ever (2 Thess. 1:9).

The self-centredness of Cain's descendants

The final result of Cain's self-centredness was that it was perpetuated in his descendants (Gen. 4:17-24).

Cain built a city and named it after his son, Enoch. There humanistic culture flourished. One of Cain's descendants, Lamech, gives us an indication of the downward trend of humanism. First, he perverted God's ideal for marriage by introducing polygamy, and then he followed in Cain's footsteps by killing a young man. But while Cain at least showed some sorrow over killing Abel, Lamech actually boasted about the murder he had committed by composing a poem about it (Gen. 4:23-24).

Self-centred, humanistic living always leaves a terrible legacy. It always leads to sexual perversion, the breakdown of the family and to violence. Why? The answer is not hard to find. When men become obsessed with themselves and refuse to live according to the laws of God, all that counts is for them to get their own way regardless of the cost.

Each and every person naturally follows the way of Cain. Thank God, there is an escape from that way. God has provided through the Lord Jesus Christ the way for us to renounce our self-centred living and put God back at the centre. What God did in Jesus can count for you if you will only repent of your sins and put your faith and trust in God's way of salvation.

2.
Esau: a warning against living for the present

Genesis 25:29-34

One of the characteristics of our age is instant gratification, that is, living for the present. In Esau we have a perfect example of this kind of mentality. Esau sold his birthright to his brother Jacob in order to satisfy his hunger.

The birthright

If we are to understand the action of Esau, we must begin with the birthright. The first-born son held a position of special prominence in most of the cultures of that time. Not only was he next to his parents in honour and authority, but the legal continuation of the family line was reckoned through him. In addition, he received a double portion of his father's inheritance. If, for instance, a man had two sons, his estate would be divided into three parts and the older son would receive two. If there were three sons, the estate would be divided into four parts, of which the oldest son would receive two.

While the birthright brought special honour and privileges in all the nations of that time, it should have had even more significance for Esau and Jacob. God had made a special covenant with their grandfather Abraham (Gen. 12:1-3). That covenant not only included the promise that the land of Canaan would belong to Abraham's descendants; it also carried the promise that a Redeemer, the Messiah himself, would spring from Abraham's seed. These promises were part and parcel of the birthright.

There were, then, two aspects of the birthright, the physical and the spiritual, and these aspects made it a most glorious and blessed privilege. Neither Jacob nor Esau rightly prized the birthright. Judging from the interest he later manifested in material prosperity, we are probably justified in saying Jacob's interest in the birthright was motivated more by the material aspect of possessing the land of Canaan than by the spiritual aspect. Jacob, of course, came to prize the spiritual aspect, but that was years later.

The bargain

But if Jacob valued only one aspect of the birthright, it is obvious that Esau prized none of it, and that brings us to consider the bargain he made.

Esau and Jacob were as different as any two men can be. Esau was a man of the outdoors and a sportsman. If he were around today, he would either be engaged in sports, talking about sports, or watching sports on TV, and would have the women swooning over him. Jacob, on the other hand, was a plain, mild-mannered man who despised physical exertion and relied on his wits to get ahead.

On the day described in this passage, the personalities of Esau and Jacob come through powerfully. Esau has been hunting while Jacob has been at home cooking a stew. With his shrewd ability to think things out, to plan ahead and to discern how others would react in a given situation, it is entirely likely that Jacob had planned for this occasion. He knew Esau was a man of impulse who did not really value his birthright and that he would return from his hunt so famished that he would do anything for food. So Jacob made sure he had a hearty stew cooked to perfection and waiting for Esau.

When Esau arrived on the scene it was immediately obvious to Jacob that he had planned well. Sure enough, Esau was famished and did not waste any time demanding some of the stew, and Jacob wasted no time in offering Esau the deal he had hatched: the stew in exchange for the birthright. Quick as a flash, Esau agreed, ate the stew and walked away.

The significance of the bargain

The deal itself actually had no bearing on the eventual possession of the birthright. We find later that Isaac was still planning to give the blessing of the first-born to Esau, and that required Jacob and his mother to have to do some more shrewd manoeuvring. But the deal Jacob and Esau made did accurately reflect the priorities and the character of these two men. It revealed Jacob's deceitfulness — a trait God worked long and hard to purge from him — and it revealed a terrible and tragic flaw in Esau.

What was Esau's flaw? Why did he so lightly regard something of such tremendous value? The answer is that he was a man who lived for the moment. The birthright to him was something distant and shadowy, something that might never be realized at all. His hunger, on the other hand, was then and there, real and pressing. He says, 'Look, I am about to die; so what is this birthright to me?' (Gen. 25:32).

That was, of course, a monstrous exaggeration. Esau was not in imminent danger of starvation, as his words implied. A man who could return to his camp lugging game with him, as Esau had done, surely had enough strength to wait for a meal to be prepared. But the point is that Esau felt at that particular moment that he was desperate for food, and that feeling was all that mattered to him. The Scottish preacher Hugh Black says of Esau, 'He feels he is going to die, as a man of his type is always sure he will die if he does not get what he wants when the passion is on him.'[1] The passion of the moment is all that counts! Instant gratification — that was Esau's mind-set.

There is, of course, no shortage of applications to be made here. Young people feel sexual passion and allow the feeling of that moment to cause them to disregard the dreadful disease of AIDS that may spring upon them a few years later, not to mention the guilt and loss of self-respect that often come only moments later. The businessman sees the chance to get ahead if he just engages in a little sharp dealing. So he allows the desire of that moment, the desire to be successful and to have financial security, to completely obscure the possibility of an indictment for fraud. The young married couple find the desire for things to be so compelling that they plunge head over heels into debt and recklessly disregard the bankruptcy that awaits them down the way. The college student plunges the drug needle into his arm because he cannot say 'No' to the intense craving of the moment, and he completely shuts out of his mind the forthcoming ruin of his health and wealth.

I am not suggesting that the immediate consequences of sin are the only reason for avoiding it. Sin is wrong even when there are no immediate consequences involved. But the disregard for the consequences of sin is one indication that Esau's mind-set is still alive and well. Much of the knack of living happily and successfully is tied to keeping firmly in mind the future consequences of present choices. But this generation has a terrifically hard time doing this and often falls into the trap of the 'Esau flaw' — living for the moment and hoping the future will take care of itself.

The most tragic manifestation of 'the Esau flaw'

This trap, as can easily be seen from the examples I have cited, can catch us in a great variety of ways, but the most tragic of all is when we barter our eternal souls for the gratification of the moment.

The gospel of Jesus Christ is much like the birthright that Esau squandered. It offers us benefits that are unseen, intangible, distant and shadowy. It says that if we will bow before Jesus Christ as our Lord and Saviour we shall receive God's forgiveness for our sins, the Holy Spirit of God will take up residence in us to guide us and cause us to mature in the things of God, and when this life is over we shall be ushered into the presence of God and the glories of heaven. But forgiveness of sin is not something that can be seen or touched. Neither is the indwelling of the Holy Spirit. And heaven may be out there somewhere, but as far as many are concerned it is at best a distant reality. This is the mind of Esau at work, and when the gospel comes, with its glorious offers, the thinking of Esau has a way of coming in and taking over. Millions have done, and are doing, with the gospel the very same thing that Esau did with the birthright. They have turned their backs on it and walked away from it so they could eat some delicacy that the world has to offer which can only satisfy for a moment.

If you are one who is about to sell your soul for the sake of some momentary gratification, I urge you to weigh the questions of Jesus about this very matter: 'For what profit is it to a man if he gains the whole world, and loses his own soul? Or what will a man give in exchange for his soul?' (Matt. 16:26).

Look at all this world has to offer and then look at the vast, boundless reaches of an eternity that will be spent either in heaven or hell. Are you ready to trade the eternal well-being of your soul in heaven for something that brings only temporary gratification? That is exactly what you do when you stop your ears against the gospel and walk away.

The author of Hebrews tells us that Esau came to regret his decision only after it was too late to do anything about it. He says, 'For you know that afterward, when he wanted to inherit the blessing, he was rejected, for he found no place for repentance, though he sought it diligently with tears' (Heb. 12:17).

I hope you will not repeat Esau's tragic blunder but that you will understand how inestimably precious the gospel is and will embrace it before it is too late. Don't let the passions and appetites of the moment blind you to eternal realities. Those realities may seem dim and distant now, but they will become real and present much sooner than you think.

3.
The Philistines: a warning against fighting God

1 Samuel 5:1-12

It was one of the darkest days in the history of the nation of Israel, a day of grim despair. As the word filtered through the towns and villages of the nation, the people must surely have reeled at the magnitude of what had happened. Their army had not only sustained staggering losses, but their sacred ark had been seized by the Philistines and carried off as a spoil of war.

In addition to these calamities, Israel had lost three of her priests. Hophni and Phinehas had died on the battlefield and their father Eli, the high priest, had died when, from the shock of the nation's resounding defeat, he had fallen off the stool he was sitting on and broken his neck.

Eli's daughter-in-law, the wife of Phinehas, best summarized the feeling of utter dismay that fell upon Israel because of the events of that day. Immediately after she gave birth to a son, she died with the sombre instruction on her lips to name him 'Ichabod', which means 'inglorious'. Why did she choose such a melancholy name? The dying mother explained it in these words: 'The glory has departed from Israel!' (1 Sam. 4:21).

The Philistines, on the other hand, were feeling quite pleased with themselves. Their army had at first been terrified when they learned that the ark of God had arrived on the battlefield.

The God of Israel was, after all, well known for the great and mighty things which he had done in Egypt before Pharaoh finally decided to free the people of Israel from bondage. But after their initial dismay, the Philistine soldiers became more determined than before, and they ended up winning the battle and bringing the ark home with them.

Their victory brought euphoria to the whole nation. As far as the Philistines were concerned, this triumph signalled the end of their hated enemies. The Israelites had, as it were, pulled out all the stops by bringing the ark of the covenant to the battlefield, but even that had not kept them from going down in humiliating defeat.

The Philistines saw their victory as proof that the God of Israel was not as powerful as they had been led to believe and that their god, Dagon, was in fact far superior. Since their god had won the victory over Israel's God, it seemed most fitting to place the ark of the covenant in the temple of Dagon (1 Sam. 5:1-2).

There are a couple of vital lessons for us to learn from this passage. The first may be put in this way: God is not defeated even though he may appear to be.

The God who cannot be defeated

The euphoria of the Philistines did not last long. They thought they had defeated the God of Israel, but they were in for a rude shock. When on the next morning they went to the temple of their false god, they found he had toppled off his stand.

How embarrassing! The first night the conquered God was in the house of the conquering god, the latter fell flat on his face! And the way in which he fell was particularly embarrassing — face down before the ark of God, as if he were paying homage to it (v. 3).

We might have thought this would have been enough to cause even these hardened Philistines to think, but they quickly dismissed any doubts that may have begun to arise in their minds, promptly seized their god and set him back in his place (v. 3). Imagine worshipping a god who had to be helped up off the floor!

The following morning was to prove even more embarrassing. When the Philistines arrived in Dagon's temple, they were distressed to find that he had once again fallen prostrate before the ark, and this time his head and his hands were broken off (v. 4). The seemingly conquered God of Israel had not been conquered at all.

We have false gods aplenty today. They are not as patently silly and foolish as an image that is half-human and half-fish, like Dagon. We are far too sophisticated for that, but our gods are no less false because they are sophisticated. Just as the Philistines of those far-off days were eager to sound the death-knell of the nation of Israel and the God of Israel, so the devotees of today's false gods are eager to sound the death-knell of Christianity and her God. And it often appears that Christianity is indeed on its last legs and that the God of the Bible has been conquered.

But many who have been quick to trumpet the death of Christianity have found the reports of her demise to be premature. Voltaire, the French philosopher who died in 1778, said Christianity would become extinct within one hundred years. It is a delicious irony that the Geneva Bible Society used his press and his house to publish large numbers of Bibles only fifty years after his death.[1]

Another example of this very same thing is the edict of Diocletian in A.D. 303 which called for the destruction of Christians and the Bible. Twenty-five years later Diocletian's successor, Constantine, commissioned Eusebius to prepare fifty Bibles at the government's expense.[2]

Yet another example is the prevailing attitude towards Christianity in England in the early 1700s. Bishop Joseph Butler observed that scepticism had become so widespread that Christianity was treated as though 'it was now discovered to be fictitious ... and nothing remained but to set it up as the subject of mirth and ridicule'.[3] But Christianity rose from that low ebb to spectacular vitality through the ministries of George Whitefield and John and Charles Wesley.

These episodes and many like them led Bernard Ramm to observe: 'A thousand times over, the death-knell of the Bible has been sounded, the funeral procession formed, the inscription cut on the tombstone, and the committal read. But somehow the corpse never stays put.'[4]

How these things should encourage and hearten every believer in Jesus Christ! No matter how bleak the times, no matter how wolfish the devil's wolves or how sheepish the Lord's sheep, God's cause is ultimately going to triumph.

The God who gives sufficient evidence

A second lesson for us to draw from this passage is that the God who cannot be defeated is also the God who has given more than sufficient evidence to win us over.

After Dagon took his second tumble we might expect to read that one Philistine said, 'This really clinches it. We can't go on believing in a god that can't even stand up on its own two feet. Let's get this useless statue out of here!' Or we might have expected someone else to say, 'The fact that Dagon never fell before we brought the Israelites' ark in here indicates that their God is greater than ours, even though we won the battle.' We might well have expected someone to go even further and say, 'I think we should investigate their God more fully.'

But, incredibly enough, no one said any of these things. Instead of renouncing their false god and turning to the true

God, they proceeded to declare the place where Dagon's head had fallen a holy place and they made a rule that no one should step on it! (1 Sam. 5:5). The Philistines saw before their eyes indisputable evidence that their god was false, and compelling evidence that the God of Israel was the true God; yet they decided to set their god up again and carry on worshipping him as if nothing had happened.

Dagon's downfall should have been enough to convince them that they were on the wrong track, but God had not finished piling on the evidence. They soon began to break out in huge, painful boils (v. 6). They simply ignored Dagon's two falls, but boils are extremely hard to ignore. This newest problem wrung from them the admission that the God of Israel was indeed at work in their midst (v. 7), but their response to this was to send the ark away to their neighbouring province (v. 8).

These Philistines may seem very dense to us, but the sad truth is that, without realizing it, many today are caught in the Philistine syndrome. This syndrome consists of ignoring the evidence as long as possible and, when it can no longer be ignored, trying to stay completely away from it.

The evidence continues to accumulate on all sides that the false gods of our own day are not working. They have neither the wisdom nor the power to deal with man's fundamental need of a new heart, but most of their followers adamantly refuse to face up to their failure. Even as the evidence piles up, these followers carry on going about the business of propping up their false gods. Here is an example. Even as evidence abounds that we are not basically good at heart and cannot be educated into good behaviour, worshippers at the shrine of education continue to insist that just a little more of it will finally make us into dazzling specimens of morality and virtue. Education has, of course, a vital role to play, but it has yet to change a sinner into a saint. Only the Spirit of God can do that.

On top of the evidence of failed gods is the evidence for the truth of Christianity. In comparison with the evidence we have for this truth, the evidence the Philistines saw may be compared to a dim beam from a tiny penlight on a foggy night.

What is this evidence for the truth of Christianity? There is fulfilled prophecy. There is that supreme evidence, the resurrection of Jesus Christ. There is the amazing survival of the Christian church despite numerous efforts to wipe it from the face of the earth. There are the testimonies of multitudes to the transforming power of Jesus Christ. There are the daily confirmations in our society of the truth of the Bible's moral principles.

What is your response to the failures of the gods of today? What is your response to all the evidence for Christianity? You can, like the Philistines of old, ignore all this evidence or try to push it away. You can send Christian witnesses away, and you can choose to stay away from the churches where the evidence for the truth of the Christian gospel is preached and taught. Or, by the grace and power of God, you can break the Philistine syndrome and accept the evidence. The one thing you cannot do is successfully fight against God. You may claim victory over him, but you can never defeat him. You can run from him, but you can never escape him.

The course of wisdom, therefore, is to throw down your arms and stop your running. Listen carefully to what the almighty God has to say about you. Listen to what he has to say about your sinful condition. Listen to what he has to say about the eternal condemnation that awaits all sinners. And when you hear these things, listen gladly to what he says about a perfect salvation that delivers from sin and judgement, a salvation that is available through the Lord Jesus Christ. Turn from your sins today. Embrace Christ as the only hope of salvation and through him find perfect peace with God.

4.
Jeroboam: an example of
falling into the 'convenience' trap

1 Kings 11:38; 12:26-33

Jeroboam was a king with a brand-new kingdom on his hands. The kingdom of Saul, David and Solomon was no more. Solomon had died and his son Rehoboam had come to the throne. The people had pleaded with him to lighten the load of demands his father had placed upon them, but Rehoboam had flatly refused. The ten northern tribes had responded to Rehoboam's refusal by forming their own kingdom, Israel, and they had chosen Jeroboam to be their king (1 Kings 12:1-20).

This division in the kingdom was not, however, simply a matter of Rehoboam's stubbornness. That was just the last straw that broke the camel's back. It all started with his father, Solomon, the king who was famous for his great wisdom. This wise man did some very foolish things. First, in direct disobedience to God's laws, he married many wives from foreign countries. Secondly, he built temples and altars in Jerusalem for the gods of his foreign wives. Finally, as if he had not done enough, he went so far as to join his wives in the worship of their heathen deities. Solomon seems to have had something of our modern era in him as well. Our age has been noted for its belief in pluralism — the notion that no one religion can claim absolute truth — and Solomon practised it to the hilt.

Because of Solomon's idolatry God had declared that he would tear the kingdom into two parts — one part going to Solomon's son, Rehoboam, and the other part going to

Jeroboam (1 Kings 11). God does not act in judgement without first giving a warning; nor, if men refuse to heed, does he
give a warning without following it up by acting in judgement,
and all things had happened just as he had said they would.

Jeroboam's problem

That, then, is how Jeroboam came to have a new kingdom on
his hands. But Jeroboam also had a problem on his hands. It is
one thing to receive a kingdom; it is quite another to sustain it.
How could he keep his fledgling kingdom going? His citizens
still had strong ties to Solomon's temple in Jerusalem and to
the great annual festivals conducted there. Jeroboam feared it
would only be a matter of time before those strong ties pulled
his people away from him and back to the house of David
(1 Kings 12:26).

Jeroboam's fear was unfounded. The same God who had
promised that he would reign over the ten tribes of Israel had
also promised that his kingdom would endure if he faithfully
and diligently obeyed God's commandments (1 Kings 11:38).
Jeroboam had seen the first promise come true, but he doubted
that the God who had fulfilled the first would, or could, fulfil
the second and give him an enduring kingdom. The only way
Jeroboam could see that part of the prophecy coming true
was through his finding a way to wean his people away from
Jerusalem.

One option was just to issue a decree, but Jeroboam knew
that would come across as a heavy-handed tactic and might
even drive the people back to Rehoboam. He had to find another way, one that would appeal to the people and make them
want to stay in Israel. He had to find a rationale that would be
sufficient to cause the people to make a substantive change in
their religious habits.

Jeroboam's solution

At last he had it! He would tell the people it was 'too much' for them to go all the way to Jerusalem to worship (1 Kings 12:28). In other words, he would tell them that their own convenience was a sufficient basis for making their religious choices. He was not really concerned about the people's convenience. Preserving his kingdom was all that mattered to Jeroboam. But he clearly thought the convenience of the people was a sufficient rationale for asking them to change their religious activities.

Jeroboam knew that if he were to convince the people that going to Jerusalem was too inconvenient for them, he must provide some form of religious activity right there in Israel that was convenient and appealing. So he decided to construct a religion of convenience.

The golden calves

First, he had two golden calves, or bulls, constructed and placed — one at Bethel, which was on the road to Jerusalem, and the other at Dan, which was in the northernmost part of the kingdom. It is clear that Jeroboam did not intend the people to think of these calves as new gods, but rather as aids for worshipping the true God (1 Kings 12:28).

This was not in fact the first time the people of God had made use of a golden calf in their worship of God. Aaron had constructed one for the people while Moses was on Mt Sinai receiving the Ten Commandments. The calf seemed to both Aaron and Jeroboam to be an appropriate symbol for the God who had demonstrated his power in bringing their forefathers out of bondage in Egypt. What Jeroboam failed to see, however, was that the calf could represent only one aspect of God, and that in only a most limited way.

The new priesthood

Secondly, he ordained priests for his two new shrines. The law of God demanded that the priests come from the tribe of Levi, but the Levites had stayed in Jerusalem to handle the rituals of the temple. So Jeroboam simply broke down the barriers of the priesthood and allowed any who wanted to be priests to serve (1 Kings 12:31).

The annual feast

Finally, Jeroboam established a great annual feast that would take the place of the festival that was instituted to commemorate Israel's deliverance from Egypt, the Passover Feast (1 Kings 12:32).

The problem with Jeroboam's solution

Jeroboam's religion was finally in place. The people had a new and exciting way of worshipping God through the calves. They had a new and unrestricted priesthood and a new festival. And it was all so convenient! Now there was no need to undertake arduous journeys to Jerusalem; they could now worship at shrines which were easy to reach. The cult of convenience had arrived!

There was only one very big problem. The Lord God whom they purported to be worshipping had some very definite ideas of his own about worship, and golden calves, a cheap priesthood and a new festival had no part in his plan. We shall never know exactly how it would have been possible for Jeroboam to sustain his new kingdom with the people continuing to worship in Jerusalem, but because God is as good as his promises we can rest assured he would have made it possible. Had

Jeroboam been willing to trust God, the people of Israel would have been able to continue in the God-ordained worship at Jerusalem while maintaining their own separate kingdom. We, of course, cannot see how that would have been possible, but it is not for us to see how God will do what he has promised, but simply to trust him to do it.

Jeroboam, of course, refused to trust God. Even though God had demonstrated the trustworthiness of his promises, Jeroboam faltered in faith. And because of that he forfeited the promise and his kingdom did not endure. After Jeroboam died, his son Nadab succeeded him and reigned for two years. Then a man named Baasha not only killed him and seized his throne but also completely exterminated all his family (1 Kings 15:25-30).

The lesson from Jeroboam

The story of Jeroboam stands, then, as a lasting reminder to trust God's promises, obey his commandments and avoid spiritual short cuts out of the desire for convenience. We badly need this reminder because we live in a time when people put a premium on convenience. We have convenience shopping. We pick up the phone and order goods which are delivered to our door. We go to the bank and we find automated cash dispensers that allow us to bank at all hours of the day and night. In the USA the drive-through mania has even led some funeral directors to use it as a means for people to pay their last respects to departed friends.

This demand for convenience has not been lost on church leaders, and in the last few years they have been falling over themselves to get the churches into a convenience mode. We want our buildings to be easily accessible, parking spaces to be plentiful and conveniently near the building, and services to start at times most people prefer. Conveniences of this kind are wonderful and are to be encouraged. But there is also a great danger with the convenience mentality. We can start regarding as matters of convenience things that God regards as necessities or non-negotiable.

This is, in fact, what many have done. They have allowed their desire for convenience so to override everything else that they feel completely free to change or even to omit altogether anything that is not convenient. George Barna says, 'A massive realignment of thinking is taking place in which people are transferring many elements formerly deemed "necessary" into the realm of the "optional". And, of course, the optional then becomes a personal matter, which many people might choose to define as desirable, but inconsequential. Church attendance, Bible reading, prayer, worship, involvement in a local church body — all of these appear to be in transition, shifting from the necessary to the optional.'[1]

It is very easy to fall into this trap. Many have an earnest desire to see Christianity advance, but they are keenly aware that many find its doctrines to be too narrow and its demands too heavy. So they start taking a nip here and a tuck there. When someone expresses alarm they have ready answers: 'We can't expect the people of today to be as committed to the church as their fathers and grandfathers were. This is a different day and age. Times have changed and we had better change along with them or we shall be past history!' The logic seems sound, but if we listen carefully we can hear in it the whisper of Jeroboam: 'Set up the golden calves!'

Please don't misunderstand me! Yes, there are many, many aspects of church life in which we can be legitimately concerned about convenience, but not in those areas where God calls for commitment and obedience. There are times when it is not convenient to attend church, but God commands that we do. There are times when it is not convenient to tell the truth, but God commands that we do. There are times when it is not convenient to forgive those who offend us, but God commands that we do.

As we live in this day which craves convenience we must remember that there is much about Christianity which is not convenient and which we are not free to change. Right at the centre of Christianity stands a cross. It was not convenient for Jesus Christ to leave the glories of heaven and become a man. It was not convenient for him to endure the hostility of wicked men. It was not convenient for him to be whipped, spat upon and ridiculed. It was not convenient to die on that cross. But he, out of love and obedience to the Father, did it all for our redemption, and he now says to each and every one who would be his follower, 'If anyone desires to come after me, let him deny himself, and take up his cross, and follow me' (Matt. 16:24).

May God help those of us who are his followers to realize that the servant is not greater than his Master. If the Lord Jesus Christ was inconvenienced for us, we should be willing to be inconvenienced for him.

5.
Jeroboam: the folly of
trying to divide or hide from God

1 Kings 14:1-12

Jeroboam was a man with a problem. His son, Abijah, was ill, critically ill.

There was a prophet of God living in Shiloh, Ahijah by name. This was the same prophet who had sought Jeroboam out some years before to tell him that God was going to take part of the kingdom away from the house of David and give it to Jeroboam (1 Kings 11:29-39).

That prophecy had come true to the letter. After Solomon died his son Rehoboam came to the throne. Rehoboam had the opportunity to soothe tempers ruffled by his father. All he had to do was to pledge that he would be an understanding and gentle shepherd for his people. But Rehoboam adamantly refused and, just as Ahijah the prophet had foretold, ten tribes of the kingdom broke away from him and made Jeroboam their king (1 Kings 12:1-20).

It comes as no surprise, therefore, that in his time of grief and trouble, Jeroboam would seek out this prophet. The surprise comes in how he went about it.

He did not go himself but sent his wife. This may very well come as only a mild surprise to us. Many men have used their wives to do work they themselves should have done. Here is the really shocking thing: Jeroboam not only asked his wife to go in his place, but to disguise herself. She was to go to the prophet in the guise of a peasant woman and, after receiving the prophetic word, give the prophet the kind of gift a peasant would bring (1 Kings 14:3).

Reasons for Jeroboam's strategy

What was going on here? Why, in the light of the great crisis in Jeroboam's life, would he not go himself? Why did he ask his wife to disguise herself?

Political implications

A couple of things come very easily and readily to mind. For one thing, Jeroboam had political implications to consider.

Shortly after he became king over the ten tribes that broke away from Rehoboam, Jeroboam had invented a whole new religion, as we saw in the previous chapter. He had placed golden calves at Bethel and Dan, had created a whole new priesthood and an annual feast and had urged the people to worship at these new shrines rather than at Jerusalem (1 Kings 12:26-33).

Now Jeroboam's son was seriously ill, and the nation was watching. If Jeroboam or his wife had been seen going to the prophet Ahijah, all the people of Israel would know that Jeroboam had created a religion that he himself did not believe in, that he had created a religion he knew to be false.

The guilt factor

Then there was the guilt factor. When Ahijah told Jeroboam that he was to be king over the ten tribes of Israel, the prophet had expressly warned Jeroboam to avoid at all costs any repetition of the sin that had caused the division of the kingdom

— that is, disobedience to God's commandments (1 Kings 11:38).

The dust stirred up by the division of the kingdom into two parts had scarcely had time to settle before Jeroboam built his calves in direct violation of the laws of God and the warning of Ahijah (1 Kings 12:25-29).

How could Jeroboam now face the prophet without hearing a stern reprimand about the course he had followed? Jeroboam also knew the same reprimand would come if the prophet recognized his wife. The disguise, therefore, was not only designed to keep the people from knowing that their king was seeking the prophet, but was also designed to keep the prophet from knowing with whom he was dealing.

The folly of Jeroboam's strategy

The utter folly of this strategy is so transparent that we can barely suppress a chuckle as we read the account. The disguise might have been effective in keeping the people from knowing what was going on, but it was totally absurd to expect the prophet to see into the future and yet not be able to see through a disguise.

When Jeroboam's wife arrived at the prophet's house she quickly discovered that her disguise was absolutely pointless and useless. The prophet was now blind (something of which she and her husband were evidently unaware, 1 Kings 14:4), but that was not what made her disguise pointless. While she was still on the doorstep, the prophet identified her (v. 6). How was he was able to do this? The Lord told him she was coming (v. 5). Prophets do not need eyes when their Master's all-discerning eye sees into the deepest crevices of the human heart.

In addition to giving Ahijah the identity of his disguised visitor, the Lord also gave him 'bad news' to declare to her

(v. 6). Because of Jeroboam's flagrant rebellion against the Lord, his house would be completely obliterated (v. 10), and the son she came to enquire about would die as soon as she returned home (v. 12). Sin carries such a heavy price!

As we scrutinize this pathetic account of Jeroboam's wife going in disguise to the prophet, we see the twin perils this man Jeroboam had fallen into at this point.

The peril of trying to divide God

First, we see Jeroboam seeking to divide God. He wanted God's compassion for the situation in which he found himself, but he did not want to live in obedience to God's commandments. In other words, he wanted God's blessing without having to live up to his demands. He wanted the God of mercy without having to acknowledge the God of justice and holiness.

Jeroboam has long since passed off the stage of history, but this business of trying to divide God is still very much alive. Preachers fall into this trap when they proclaim a message that emphasizes only the love of God and that conveniently ignores our sin, the wrath of God upon that sin and the heartfelt, radical repentance that is necessary to deal with it.

There is, in other words, a very popular message going out today that seeks to rob God of his holiness. It is a message that says God is prepared to save people without any regard to his holiness at all. Those who proclaim this message see only one thing in the cross of Christ, and that is the love of God. As far as they are concerned, that is all the cross means.

But look again at that cross. There the Lord Jesus is suffering untold anguish and pain. As he hangs there the blackest darkness imaginable falls over the land and he cries out: 'My God, my God, why have you forsaken me?' (Matt. 27:46). Why? What was the reason for this darkness and this piercing cry? The answer of the apostle Paul to that great question is that the cross allowed God the Father to be 'just and the justifier of the one who has faith in Jesus' (Rom. 3:26). The cross was God's answer to this crushing dilemma: how could God satisfy his justice by punishing guilty sinners and yet at the same time satisfy his grace by letting those same sinners go free?

The cross allowed God to do both. It satisfied his justice in that sin was punished there. The Lord Jesus Christ had no sins of his own, but he bore the penalty of others. But grace was also satisfied because justice demands that the penalty for sin be paid only once, and if Jesus paid that penalty there is nothing left for the believing sinner to pay.

Let us never forget that the cross of Christ answers the demands of both justice and grace. It is a mighty demonstration of the love of God for guilty sinners, but it is not love at the expense of God's holiness. God does not save sinners by throwing his holiness out of the window. He saves them in a holy way. The love manifested in that cross can never be appreciated until we see it against the backdrop of God's wrath. Here is how much he loved guilty sinners — enough to pour out his wrath on his own Son instead of on the sinners!

The love of Calvary is a holy love, and preachers who fail to see this repeat Jeroboam's error, as do those who embrace their message.

Even those of us who profess to know Christ can fall into the trap of trying to divide God. We do so when we when we subscribe to the notion that a person can be truly saved and not have any regard for holiness.

This notion has been very popular in recent years. It has been advanced in terms of the 'carnal Christian' teaching. This teaching maintains that there are not just Christians and non-Christians, but a third category of those who are truly saved but live as if they were lost. Those in this category have the best of both worlds. They are able to enjoy all the pleasures of sin in this life and still go to heaven when they die.

The only problem is that there is no such category. While it is true that Christians can and do slip into carnal, sinful behaviour from time to time in their lives, that is a far cry from continually living in sin, something the Bible clearly states is impossible for the child of God (1 John 3:9). On the other hand, the Bible affirms that all who truly believe have been created in Christ Jesus 'for good works' (Eph. 2:10) and that anyone who claims to have faith apart from such works has only dead faith (James 2:14-26). In addition to these things, the Lord Jesus himself taught that his disciples will continue, not in sin, but in faith in him and in obedience to his Word (John 8:31; 15:6-8).

It is possible, of course, to reject the 'carnal Christian' theory and still become ensnared in the trap that Jeroboam fell into. Those who are truly children of God can separate the blessings of God from obedience to his commands. How often we do this! We want God to pour out his blessings on our lives, and yet we play fast and loose with his commandments.

The peril of hiding from God

The second peril into which Jeroboam fell may be termed hiding from God. While acknowledging Ahijah as a prophet of the living God, Jeroboam, incredibly and inexplicably, thought he could succeed in concealing his wife's identity. On one hand he acknowledged God, while denying him on the other hand.

This peril remains with us just as much as the other. Multitudes acknowledge God while trying to hide from him. They know he is out there and that they must some day come before him and give account of themselves. But they vainly imagine that they can stand before him with their true selves hidden from his view.

The Bible constantly thunders out the message that we are all sinners by nature and we cannot hope to enter heaven unless our sins are forgiven. It further insists that our sins can only be dealt with through the redeeming work of the Lord Jesus Christ, that through that work he has provided us with the perfect garment of his righteousness.

But in the face of this clear message, many refuse to deal with their sins. They think they can put the cloak of good works over their sinful nature and God will never know it. Or perhaps they think they can put the cloak of church membership over that sinful nature and God will be fooled.

Matthew Henry observes: 'Those who think by their disguises to hide themselves from God will be wretchedly confounded when they find themselves disappointed in the day of discovery. Sinners now appear in the garb of saints, and are taken to be such; but how they will blush and tremble when they find themselves stripped of their false colours, and are called by their own name: "Go out, thou treacherous false-hearted hypocrite. *I never knew thee. Why feignest thou thyself to be another?*" Tidings of a portion with hypocrites will be heavy tidings. God will judge men according to what they are, not according to what they seem'[1] (italics are his).

Jeroboam suffered a terrible judgement because he foolishly thought he could divide God and hide from him. Now he shouts to us across the pages of Scripture and over the centuries. He warns us not to repeat his folly. He tells us to accept the full God — that is, the God who is not only loving but also just. And he also urges us not to disguise our sinful condition but to deal with it by accepting God's plan of salvation.

6.
Ahab: the danger of 'feel-good' religion

1 Kings 22:1-8,13-14

Ahab, King of Israel, had made up his mind to take the city of Ramoth Gilead away from the Syrians. He was afraid he was not strong enough to do it by himself, so he decided to enlist the help of Jehoshaphat, King of Judah. Jehoshaphat agreed to help on the condition that Ahab first seek the mind of God on the matter.

Jehoshaphat's request posed no problem for Ahab. He had at his disposal a whole crowd of prophets who were anxious to say whatever he wanted. If he needed a green light from God on anything, all he had to do was bring in these prophets and they would all assure him that his plans were pleasing to God.

So when Jehoshaphat asked him to seek the mind of God on their plans, Ahab called in four hundred prophets and put the question to them: 'Shall I go against Ramoth Gilead to fight, or shall I refrain?' Without the slightest hesitation the prophets all promptly chorused: 'Go up, for the Lord will deliver it into the hand of the king' (1 Kings 22:6).

Jehoshaphat was not impressed. He was a deeply spiritual man and he was not interested in what a bunch of tame court prophets had to say. He wanted to hear from a man who was in touch with the living God, one who not only knew the mind of God but who would fearlessly proclaim it. So when the four hundred prophets had finished falling over themselves to say what Ahab wanted them to say, Jehoshaphat asked, 'Is there not still a prophet of the Lord here, that we may enquire of him?' (v. 7).

Ahab announces his standard for prophets

Ahab's answer to that simple question spoke volumes: 'There is still one man, Micaiah the son of Imlah, by whom we may enquire of the Lord; but I hate him, because he does not prophesy good concerning me, but evil' (v. 8).

There is no mystery about what Ahab was saying here. He did not want to bring in this solitary prophet, Micaiah, because he knew he would say something negative and disturbing, something that the king did not want to hear. In other words, Ahab was not interested in the truth. His interest was in feeling good. He was essentially saying, 'I decide what is true by how it makes me feel.'

Jehoshaphat, on the other hand, was not in the least concerned about how Micaiah made Ahab feel. He was interested in knowing whether they would return from Ramoth Gilead in one piece! So he insisted that Ahab bring in this despised prophet and hear what he had to say. Ahab reluctantly agreed and sent an officer to fetch Micaiah. This officer decided he would make sure Micaiah did not say anything unsettling or disturbing to the king. Therefore, when he located the prophet he said to him, 'Now listen, the words of the prophets with one accord encourage the king. Please, let your word be like the word of one of them, and speak encouragement' (v. 13).

Micaiah is informed of Ahab's standard

The officer was polite and respectful towards Micaiah but his message was clear. If we put it in terms we are familiar with, it amounts to this: 'Micaiah, for once, please don't rock the boat. Everyone else is agreed that the king should undertake this mission, and all we want you to do is go along with the crowd and make it unanimous.'

Micaiah's response carried both the rumble of thunder and the crack of lightning: 'As the Lord lives, whatever the Lord says to me, that I will speak' (v. 14). In other words, Micaiah was insisting that the truth was not a nose of wax that could be twisted into any shape Ahab wanted. There was such a thing as absolute truth, whether Ahab liked it or not.

After that little exchange, Micaiah was off to see the king. He and Ahab did not exchange any pleasantries. They did not talk about the weather or ask about each other's families. Ahab came right to the point: 'Micaiah, shall we go to war against Ramoth Gilead, or shall we refrain?' (v. 15).

We are at first taken aback by Micaiah's response. We expect him to answer with a resounding and stern 'No!' Surprisingly, he falls in line and says what all the other prophets had been saying: 'Go and prosper, for the Lord will deliver it into the hand of the king!' (v. 15). Why would he say such a thing? Why would he make such a fuss about speaking only the word of the Lord and then meekly repeat the 'politically correct' line? Micaiah was essentially saying to Ahab: 'All right, if you just want to hear what makes you feel good, I will say what makes you feel good.' It is not always a blessing when God gives us what we want!

Micaiah ignores Ahab's standard

Ahab, however, had not gone to the trouble of bringing Micaiah in to just hear him parrot what the other prophets were saying, so he insisted that he deliver the true message of God. No, Ahab had not had a change of heart, and he still was not interested in the truth of God. He simply wanted to confirm for

Jehoshaphat that Micaiah was just what he had declared him
to be — a man who never had anything good to say. That is
why after Micaiah spoke the word of God, namely, that Israel
would be defeated and Ahab would die in battle, Ahab did not
change his plans one iota, but merely said, 'Did I not tell you that
he would not prophesy good concerning me, but evil?' (v. 18).

Ahab ignores Micaiah's message

Ahab completely disregarded the sombre message of Micaiah
and ploughed straight ahead to his doom. Perhaps he con-
soled himself with the fact that four hundred prophets had
been favourable and only one had not. Four hundred to one —
not bad odds! But even though Micaiah was outnumbered, his
prophecy came true. Israel was defeated and Ahab died, just
as he had said (vv. 29-40).

Poor, blind Ahab! He thought the trouble was with Micaiah,
that Micaiah was a man who just enjoyed being negative and
harsh. It never dawned on Ahab that Micaiah was just faithfully telling him the truth of God. Micaiah had no desire to be
harsh or cruel to Ahab. On the contrary, Micaiah's message
was designed for Ahab's ultimate good. If he had listened to
Micaiah's message, Ahab could either have prevented the dis-
aster that was about to befall him and the nation, or at the very
least have prepared himself to meet God. But because he
thought Micaiah was just a negative man with a harsh message and that he could choose to believe the message that made
him feel good, he ended up losing everything.

Other examples of Ahab's mentality

There are plenty of other examples in the Bible of people who
did exactly the same as Ahab and ignored the word of God

because it disturbed them and did not make them feel good. The people of Samuel's day wanted to be like all the other nations and have their own king. They disregarded the clearly expressed will of God and selected Saul. That made them all feel very good for a while, but in the long run it was a choice that brought great pain to their nation (1 Sam. 8).

Then there was the small remnant of people who were left in Judah after the Babylonians carried most of the population into captivity. This remnant approached the prophet Jeremiah to ask if it was God's will for them to go to Egypt. Jeremiah emphatically responded that it was God's will for them to remain in the land of Judah. That was not, however, what the people wanted to hear. It upset them and disturbed them, and they said to Jeremiah, 'As for the word that you have spoken to us in the name of the Lord, we will not listen to you! But we will certainly do whatever has gone out of our own mouth' (Jer. 44:16-17).

The thought of leaving the ruin and devastation of Judah behind and going to Egypt made these people feel good for a time. They may very well have made their journey there with a great deal of hilarity and frivolity. Little did they know that they were marching into the very same thing they had left behind in Judah. Many of them met the death in Egypt they had managed to avoid in Judah (Jer. 44:24-30).

The continuing temptation of 'feel-good' religion

The sad saga of people wanting to feel good and refusing to listen to anything that makes them feel bad continues to this very day and hour. The message of Christianity has some very stern and disturbing aspects to it. It tells us that we are all sinners, and that we must some day stand before a holy and righteous God and give account of ourselves. It further tells us that if we stand before this holy God in our sins he will send us into everlasting destruction. These are not teachings that make us leap into the air with joy and eager anticipation. And because they are disturbing teachings, many simply ignore the message and look for a message that is more to their liking, stubbornly refusing to accept the idea that there is such a thing as absolute truth. How do they decide what is true and what is not? A great number of them say with Ahab, 'I decide what is true by how it makes me feel!'

And there is no shortage of preachers and churches who, seeing the desire of people for a message that makes them feel good, are anxious to supply it. One denomination conducted a nationwide campaign to attract new members by using this slogan: 'Instead of me fitting a religion, I found a religion to fit me.' There are echoes of Ahab here: 'I don't have to listen to Micaiah if he causes me to be depressed.'

We would never think of employing such reasoning with our physical health. If your doctor were to say you had a life-threatening illness that must be treated, you would not think of accusing him or her of being negative and harsh. You would understand that the doctor had your best interests at heart, and you would embrace the negative diagnosis in order to secure the positive result of good health. On the other hand, you would not think of going to a doctor who had the repu-tation of telling people what they wanted to hear while all the time some disease was ravaging their bodies. When it comes to our physical health, we want the truth even if it hurts.

We should take the same approach to our spiritual health. Christianity, as we have seen, does have a very negative diag-nosis of our spiritual condition but, thank God, that diagnosis is intended to yield a positive result. Yes, the Bible tells us about our sins and God's forthcoming judgement, but it also tells us that there is in the perfect life and the atoning death of Jesus Christ a cure for our sins. Until we face the negative truths about ourselves we shall never be able to embrace the positive truths about the all-sufficient Saviour, Jesus Christ.

'Feel-good' religion is running at flood-tide today. The question we must all ruthlessly ask ourselves is this: 'What value is there in a religion that says what I want to hear if I end up losing my eternal soul?'

7.

Amaziah: the folly of explaining away a message from God

Amos 7:10-17

This passage brings before us a man named Amaziah. He is identified as 'the priest of Bethel' (Amos 7:10). When we see the word 'priest', we usually think of a priest of the Lord, but this man was far from that. Bethel was the place where, as we read in chapter 4, a former King of Israel, Jeroboam, had set up the worship of a golden calf (1 Kings 12:28-29). Now another Jeroboam (Amos 7:10) was on the throne of Israel, and the idolatrous worship of this calf at Bethel continued unabated.

Everything seemed to be going along splendidly in the kingdom of Israel. It was a time of great prosperity and stability (Amos 3:12,15; 4:1; 6:4,6), and religion was popular and flourishing (Amos 4:4; 5:5,21-23; 8:3,10).

The peaceful tranquillity of Israel did not last long. A sheep-breeder and tender of sycamore fruit (Amos 7:14) from Israel's sister kingdom, Judah, suddenly burst on the scene with a clear and disturbing message from God. This man, Amos, came storming into Israel's complacent life to declare that God was irrevocably opposed to all forms of idolatry and was absolutely committed to utterly shattering the idolatrous worship of Bethel (Amos 3:13-15). In addition to this, Amos prophesied that the people of Israel would be carried away captive by a foreign nation (Amos 5:27; 6:7).

Amos' message was, then, one of God's wrath against the sin of his people and of judgement that could only be averted by sincere and thorough-going repentance.

It was a message that Amaziah found extremely agitating and upsetting, so much so that he first reported Amos to the king (Amos 7:10-11) and then confronted the prophet himself (vv. 12-13).

Amaziah's grand assumption

As we look at Amaziah's words to the king and to Amos, we can quite easily spot the grand assumption that he makes: that Amos' message was not to be explained in terms of a word from God, but rather in terms of Amos' own thinking. In other words, the message was not divine in origin but was nothing more than a mere man offering his own assessment.

Because Amos' message was not, in Amaziah's view, a divine message, it could be rejected on the basis that it was unpopular ('The land is not able to bear all his words' — v. 10). It could also be rejected on the ground of pluralism. As far as Amaziah was concerned, he and his people already had their own religion, and it was very egotistical and dogmatic of Amos to insist that his way was right. And a less than divine message meant Amos could take it elsewhere! So Amaziah did not hesitate to say to Amos:

Go, you seer!
Flee to the land of Judah,
There eat bread,
And there prophesy,
But never again prophesy at Bethel...

(vv. 12-13).

The one thing that never seemed to occur to Amaziah was the possibility that Amos was not at Bethel by his own choosing, but rather because of God's direction, and that his message there was not one of his own inventing but rather one revealed by God. Amos was quick to set him straight on both points. He affirmed that it was God who 'took' him while he was following his flock, and it was God who plainly said to him, 'Go, prophesy to my people Israel' (v. 15). Had it been a matter of his own choosing, Amos would still have been happily tending his flock and his sycamore fruit, but it was a matter of God's choosing and speaking.

At first glance it may seem that the exchange between Amaziah and Amos amounts to a draw. Amaziah asserts that Amos' message is his own and Amos asserts that it is not. Are we to see this as the type of encounter in which children so often engage? One calls the other a name, the other denies it and then the first shouts back: 'Yes, you are!' and the second retorts: 'No, I'm not!' And so it goes on.

Amos' evidence

We are greatly mistaken if we see the encounter between Amaziah and Amos in this way. It was no mere childish exchange of charge and countercharge. There was solid evidence to support Amos' message.

The law of Moses

First, he could point to the law of Moses, the law under which the people of Israel were constituted as a nation, to confirm his message. It was Moses' law which soundly warned the people that devastating judgement would inevitably result from idolatry (Deut. 4:26-28; 6:13-15; 8:19-20; 30:17-18).

The experiences of their forefathers

Then Amos could point to instances of their forefathers actually experiencing severe judgement for going after idols. One such instance involved the worship of a golden calf (Exod. 32:1-6,27-28).

The experiences of his hearers

Finally, Amos could say his message had already been confirmed by what his hearers had themselves experienced. Recent drought, diseased crops, locusts and an epidemic were strong signs of God's displeasure (Amos 4:6-11).

Amaziah's blindness

With all the evidence for Amos' message, we cannot help wondering how Amaziah was able to explain it in naturalistic terms. How did he miss the authentic ring of God's voice in the midst of Amos' words? The answer seems to be that he was so much in love with his own little world that he dismissed the evidence for Amos' message. He looked at Bethel and saw there the king's sanctuary and his residence, and himself as a part of it all. His eyes were blinded to the heavenly sanctuary by an earthly sanctuary. He missed the divine character of Amos' message because he was so much in love with life in this world.

Amaziah's tragedy

It may seem that Amaziah was not guilty of anything all that significant. Many would chalk up his misreading of Amos' message as a slight mistake but not a colossal tragedy. The man whom God had called and sent to Bethel regarded Amaziah's view far differently. Because Amaziah missed the divine character of his message, Amos announced that he and his family would experience terrible heartache and woe (Amos 7:17), and Amos' words proved true, not because he just happened to make a lucky guess about Amaziah, but because his message was exactly what he claimed it to be — a message from God himself.

Today's Amaziahs

Is there any difficulty in understanding what all this has to do with us? There should not be. We all, like Amaziah, are confronted with a message that purports to be divine in origin and character. It is a message that contains unpleasant and disturbing features. It tells us that there is a holy God to whom we must give account, that this holy God burns in righteous indignation against our sins, and that he is committed to bringing eternal judgement upon all those who are found in their sins.

Thank God, this message also contains good news. This holy God with whom we have to do has made a way for our sins to be forgiven. That way is his Son, Jesus Christ. On the basis of Christ's perfect life and substitutionary death, guilty sinners can stand in God's presence clothed in the garment of the perfect righteousness of Christ.

Sadly, there are many who do with this message exactly what Amaziah did. They regard it in a naturalistic way. They see it as a message that was invented by mere men, and because of that they contend that it can safely be dismissed. If anyone finds in the Christian message anything that is disturbing, unpleasant, or unpopular he or she can merely ignore it. If anyone has a religious view that runs counter to what the gospel claims, he or she can go right ahead holding that view, because, they argue, the Christian gospel is just one message among many.

All such arguments assume, of course, that there is no evidence for the Christian gospel, that there is absolutely nothing to substantiate it as divine in origin. But fulfilled prophecies, the changed lives of millions of believers down through the centuries, the empty tomb outside Jerusalem, and many other evidences as well, all scream at us that the Christian gospel is divine in origin. Those who ignore this evidence will find, as Amaziah did, that to treat a divine message as less than divine does not destroy the message, but it does invite the wrath of God.

8.

Three men: three hindrances to following Christ

Luke 9:57-62

The middle portion of Luke's Gospel (9:51 - 19:44) recounts for us the most intriguing journey in all of human history. It tells us of our Lord's final journey to Jerusalem where he was to lay down his life to purchase eternal salvation for all who believe in him.

Most of this long section is taken up with words that Jesus spoke. But the record of his teaching is interspersed with a sprinkling of accounts of his encounters with several individuals. The rich young ruler, Bartimaeus and Zacchaeus are all here (18:18 - 19:10) among others.

The verses which form the subject of this chapter tell us of three men whom Jesus encountered in quick succession. The key word in these encounters is 'follow'. Two of these men professed their desire to follow Christ (Luke 9:57,61), while Jesus himself issued this command to the other: 'Follow me' (v. 59).

What does it mean to follow Christ? It means to become his disciple, or, to put it another way, to become a Christian. The Christian is one who follows Christ. He has stopped following his own way and now follows Christ's way. He has turned from his sins to Christ, received him as Lord and Saviour and now seeks to live according to what he commands. Christ is leading the way and the Christian is in the rear.

No Christian is a perfect follower of Christ but, make no mistake about it, every Christian is a follower. The Bible knows nothing of a non-following follower. One might as well speak of a square circle. The Christian may stray from the path of following Christ. He may lag far behind at times. He may even run ahead of his Lord from time to time but, however imperfectly he does so, he follows Christ.

The issue before us in this passage, then, is that of becoming a child of God and, tragically, these men all fell short. They teetered on the very verge of genuine discipleship, but failed finally to embrace Christ. They failed because each was in the grip of a dangerous attitude that waged war on true discipleship.

Not much has changed since the long-ago day described in these verses. Yes, these men have long since passed off the stage of human history, and the Lord Jesus Christ himself is not now ministering in the flesh as he was then. Yes, we have our computers, our cellular phones, and we can walk on the moon. But the single greatest issue facing each and every one of us is exactly the same today as it was then: what will we do with the Lord Jesus Christ, the God-man? Will we embrace him as Saviour, follow him and receive the eternal life he offers? Or will we, as these men did, turn away from him?

The same perilous attitudes that crippled the following of these men are poised to cripple would-be followers of Christ today. My hope in presenting these men and the hindrances that kept them from following Christ is to persuade my unsaved readers not to let these pernicious attitudes do the same hellish work they did in the lives of these men.

The dangers of personal ease and comfort

The first man presents us with the danger of seeking personal ease and comfort.

As Jesus journeys along, this man draws alongside and says, 'Lord, I will follow you wherever you go' (Luke 9:57).

There was nothing in the man's words to indicate a problem. His profession seems to us to be sincere, and we would have expected Jesus to welcome him aboard. But Jesus did not. The Gospel accounts frequently remind us that Jesus could read the innermost thoughts of men as easily as we read words on paper (John 2:23-25; 4:16-19)

While this man was professing his readiness to follow, Jesus was reading his thoughts and motives, and what he read there indicated that this man's words were just words.

Jesus knew this man had not counted the cost of discipleship, that he would follow him as long as it was convenient and comfortable, but at the first sign of hardship and difficulty he would abandon ship.

So Jesus replied, 'Foxes have holes and birds of the air have nests, but the Son of Man has nowhere to lay his head' (Luke 9:58).

And we read no more of this man. He did not even follow long enough to encounter hardship. Jesus' words about hardship were enough to make him vanish as quickly as he appeared.

The peril of procrastination

The second man presents us with the peril of procrastination (Luke 9:59-60).

Perhaps it was as the first man beat a hasty retreat that Jesus turned to this man and said, 'Follow me.' In other words, it may be that Jesus used the failure of the first man to challenge this man and say to him, in effect, 'How about you? Are you ready to follow me?'

The man may very well have been taken aback by Jesus' blunt command. He may even have stammered and spluttered before he regained his composure. He did not want to follow Jesus, but he knew he had to have a seemingly unanswerable excuse. At last he had it! 'Lord, let me first go and bury my father' (v. 59).

At first sight it seems to have been a perfectly legitimate excuse. Here was a man who truly wanted to follow the Lord but had an unavoidable conflict of duty. The Jews considered proper burial as the most important of all duties. It took precedence over the study of the law, the performance of temple service, the killing of the Passover lamb and the performance of the rite of circumcision.[1]

But wait! Something is not right here. If this man had to bury his father, why was he not doing it? Why was he out here by the roadside to catch a glimpse of Jesus journeying along? Burials in those days had to be tended to without delay.

The answer is that the man's father was not dead yet. The man was, then, asking Jesus to put off his demand for discipleship until his father died and was buried. It was a plea for an indefinite delay. It is obvious that this man had never really seen how vitally urgent and surpassingly important the demands of Christ are.

Jesus saw through this man as easily as he had the first. His words, 'Let the dead bury their own dead...' called him to rethink his priorities and to act decisively and quickly. There was before him a far more pressing and vital matter — namely, his own spiritual life. Those who are spiritually dead can give themselves to tending to the matters of this life. But those who have spiritual life give evidence of it by putting Christ above everything else.

After Jesus spoke these words, we read no more of this man. He evidently vanished as quickly as the first. But his error has not vanished. Many, when confronted with the message of salvation, take up the words of this foolish man: 'Lord, let me first...'

There are many murderers of souls. Doubt about the truth has slain its thousands. Love of ease and comfort has as well. But I wonder if this business of simply procrastinating will not in the final analysis prove to be the most prolific of all these murderers.

The danger of the divided heart

The third man presents us with the danger of the divided heart (vv. 61-62).

Like the first man, this fellow professed his readiness to follow Jesus, but he quickly added one condition. He must first go to bid farewell to his family.

This also seems to have been a perfectly legitimate request. Jesus had scriptural precedent for granting it. Elijah had allowed Elisha to bid farewell to his family before taking up the work to which he had been called (1 Kings 19:19-21).

But Jesus, that great reader of men's hearts, knew the two cases were not equal. Elisha's request came from a heart that was eager to follow, while this man's came from one that was reluctant to follow. To go home and bid farewell was for Elisha the way to show he was making a radical break with his old life and giving himself to his new task. But the man with whom Jesus was dealing made his request from a desire to return home to discuss and deliberate with his family whether he was doing the right thing. He had obviously not yet been seized by the same spirit that gripped Elisha, the spirit that willingly and readily took up God's call.

He was a man who harboured a divided heart. Part of him wanted to follow the Lord while another part wanted to stay at home. Many suffer from that same divided heart. They want their sins to be forgiven and to follow Christ, but they also want to hang on to the life of sin.

To all of these, Jesus delivers the same word that he gave to this man. The kingdom of God requires a whole heart. A person can no more be saved and hang on to his old life of sin and his love for the world than a farmer can plough a straight furrow by looking in the opposite direction.

How does the account of these three men find you today? Have you embraced Christ as your Saviour? Are you following him? Or are you repeating one or more of the errors of these men?

Please don't misunderstand the message of these verses. The Lord Jesus is not saying his followers cannot have any possessions or family ties. Other teachings in Scripture make it clear that this is not what Jesus meant at all. What he is teaching is this — the salvation of our souls is of such surpassing and vital importance that nothing, yes, nothing, must be put ahead of it. Personal ease and comfort must be laid aside. The tendency to procrastinate must be laid aside. Love of our old life must be put away. And the Lord Jesus must be trusted and followed. Nothing is more important.

9.

The rich young ruler: a warning against mistaken assumptions

Luke 18:18-23

As we saw in the previous chapter, the middle section of Luke's Gospel is devoted to the greatest journey in all of human history, the journey of the Lord Jesus Christ to Jerusalem to die on a Roman cross through which he would provide eternal salvation for sinners.

We are mistaken if we think Jesus was blindly marching towards calamity. He not only knew he was going to Jerusalem to die, but he also carefully orchestrated events so that his death would coincide with the Jewish Passover. He was the true Lamb of God whom the Passover lamb of the Old Testament was intended to prefigure, and it was essential, therefore, that he should die at precisely the time the Passover lambs were slain.

During the course of his journey, the Lord Jesus encountered several intriguing individuals. One of these is known to us as the rich young ruler. It is important for us to meet this young man. He reminds us of how vitally important it is for us to be right about the matter of eternal salvation. He reminds us that it is possible to be right about a great number of important issues and yet be wrong about this most important of all issues.

What he was right about

The importance of eternal life

First, we can say he was right to be urgently concerned about eternal life. As Jesus journeyed along, the young man hailed him with these words: 'Good Teacher, what shall I do to inherit eternal life?' (Luke 18:18).

There can be no doubt about the depth of his interest, about the urgency he felt about this issue. Mark's Gospel tells us that he came, not casually strolling towards Jesus, but rather running to him (Mark 10:17). That was not all. He was so vitally interested in this matter that he addressed Jesus in the presence of others (Luke 18:26). He was not embarrassed to let it be known that he wanted to have this most precious of all things, eternal life.

How different he was in comparison with our generation! Most Americans pride themselves on being prepared for every eventuality. They have insurance for their homes, their cars and their bodies. They try to plan ahead for sending their children to college. But while many are very good at preparing for these things, they give no thought at all to preparing for eternity.

The irony is that many of the things for which we diligently prepare may in fact never happen, while eternity will certainly happen. We are all going to be thrust out into eternity some day. The author of Hebrews says that it is 'appointed' for men to die and after this comes judgement (Heb. 9:27). We can safely ignore eternity only when we stop dying. But as long as we are a dying people we had better share the rich young ruler's interest in eternal life.

Coming to Jesus as the authority on eternal life

This young man was also correct to come to Jesus about this matter. Jesus is the world's foremost authority on the question of eternal life. He came to this earth from the realm of eternity (John 3:13), and he came for the express purpose of making it possible for us to enter that eternal realm from which he came. He came to give us eternal life (John 3:16). And there is eternal life in no other (John 3:36; 14:6; Acts 4:12).

Simon Peter was one who understood these truths. When a multitude were offended by the teaching of Jesus and turned away, he and the other disciples stayed with Jesus. When Jesus asked if they also wanted to depart, Peter replied, 'Lord, to whom shall we go? You have the words of eternal life' (John 6:68).

Millions today never make this connection. They look upon eternal life as the automatic possession of all without exception. Or they think it can be achieved apart from Christ. The rich young ruler was miles ahead of such people. Although he did not hear what Peter had to say about Jesus having the words of eternal life, he sensed it was true and came to Jesus.

What he was wrong about

But while he was right to be concerned about eternal life and to come to Jesus about that concern, he was sadly mistaken in three ways.

He thought Jesus was only a good teacher

First, he was wrong to think Jesus was only a 'Good Teacher' (Luke 18:18). This title was, of course, an accurate description of Jesus as far as it went. Jesus was good and he was a teacher. But accepting Jesus as a good teacher is not enough when it comes to this issue of eternal life. If Jesus were only a good teacher, there would be no eternal life for anyone.

Jesus challenged this young man at this point by asking, 'Why do you call me good? No one is good but one, that is, God' (v. 19).

What was going on here? Was Jesus denying that he was God in human flesh? No, not at all. Why would he deny here what he so explicitly affirmed on other occasions? In reality Jesus was affirming his deity. He was essentially asking, 'Do you really regard me as good in the fullest sense of the word? Are you willing to accept what that implies about me? Do you understand that if I am really good, I am no mere man, but am nothing less than God himself in human flesh?' He was essen tially saying to this young man, 'Don't call me good if you are not willing to call me "God".'

Jesus was teaching this young man that he could not have this thing he so earnestly desired, eternal life, if he was not willing to submit to him as God. The young man was right to come to Jesus about eternal life, but he had to recognize that life was not in some sort of formula Jesus had to give, but rather in Jesus himself.

All sorts of people are willing to admit part of the truth about Jesus. They are ready to acknowledge him as a good teacher and as a good moral example, but eternal life comes only to those who sincerely acknowledge him as God. The apostle John writes, 'Whoever confesses that Jesus is the Son of God, God abides in him, and he in God' (1 John 4:15).

He thought eternal life can be attained through good works

Secondly, this young man was wrong to think eternal life could be secured by good works. The Gospel of Matthew records him as asking, 'What good thing shall I do that I may have eternal life?' (Matt. 19:16). Jesus' answer to that question has been extremely puzzling and perplexing to many. He said, 'If you want to enter into life, keep the commandments' (Matt. 19:17). It seems as if Jesus was agreeing with him. The young man asked what good thing he could do, and the Lord Jesus pointed him to obeying God's commandments as the good thing he could do.

In reality Jesus was showing him how utterly helpless he was in this matter of attaining eternal life. If we could perfectly keep the commandments of God we would be righteous in his sight, but no one has ever done so except Christ. If we would be righteous in the eyes of God, then, we must not look to anything we can do but rather to the righteousness of the Lord Jesus Christ. His righteousness is applied to us when we see how perfectly helpless we are and cast ourselves unreservedly on him.

He turned away from Jesus

Finally, this young man was wrong to turn away from Jesus. After telling him to keep the commandments of God, Jesus listed five of those commandments (Luke 18:20). And the young man confidently responded: 'All these things I have kept from my youth' (v. 21). If eternal life was a matter of keeping God's commandments, he thought he was well on his way. He could not have been more wrong. The Lord Jesus told him, 'You still lack one thing. Sell all that you have and distribute to the poor, and you will have treasure in heaven; and come, follow me' (v. 22).

With these words, Jesus brought this young man face to face with the pivotal issue in this business of having eternal life. The young man thought he was willing to do anything to secure eternal life. The question was whether he was willing to do the absolutely essential and indispensable thing. Was he willing to break with his idol, material possessions, and submit to Christ, and Christ alone? We know how he answered that question. With sorrow he turned away from Christ (v. 23).

The Lord does not require us to give up all our material possessions to be saved. But he does require that we decisively break with our idols and commit ourselves to him alone as our Lord and Saviour (1 Thess. 1:9). If your idol is money, the Lord demands that you renounce it and rest solely upon him. If it is pleasure, the Lord demands that you break with it and cast yourself upon him. If it is your own preconceived notions about God and salvation, the Lord demands that you cast them aside and embrace his revealed truth. Even after we are saved, our hearts stray from time to time back to our former gods and our former way of life. But occasional straying is far different from continually serving. No one can be saved who comes to Christ with the intention to keep on serving his idols and following his sins.

When this young man heard Jesus' call to break with his god, his heart sank. He wanted eternal life, but not at the cost of giving up his god. He made his decision. What is your decision? Do you prize eternal life enough to repent of your sins and commit yourself to living under the lordship of Christ? Or will you cling to your sins and turn away from Christ?

10.
Gamaliel: the impossibility of sitting on the fence

Acts 5:27-42

If A is A, then B is not A. It was not all that long ago that almost everyone in our society understood that simple statement. But strange gremlins have invaded our thinking in recent years, and we now find people arguing that both A and B can be A. In other words, we have reached a point in which we embrace mutually exclusive options, and we argue that both sides of a contradiction can be true.

Take the most pressing moral and social issues of our day and you will find this mentality at work. Americans increasingly try to deal with these issues by having it both ways. Multitudes say they are both for and against something at the same time. They are against abortion themselves because they believe it is morally wrong, but they are for it for others. In like manner, they are against homosexuality themselves, but they are for it for others. They are against pornography for themselves, but they are for it for others. Even in theological matters we find people trying to occupy the middle ground by arguing that salvation is a matter of both grace and good works.

The reason for the attraction of the middle ground is not hard to find. It is comfortable. It requires no commitment. It frees us from unpleasant confrontations with those who hold a definite conviction. If a person agrees with everybody, nobody gets cross with him!

The middle is attractive ground to people of every age, but our age seems to find it more appealing than others. We prize peace and despise commitment and the middle ground offers the one while not requiring the other.

Meet Gamaliel. Distinguished member of the Sanhedrin Court, scholar *extraordinaire*, calm, cool and collected — that was Gamaliel. If anyone should have been gifted at sifting through evidence, drawing a clear and distinct conclusion, and acting decisively, it was he.

The conflicting propositions

But in this passage of Scripture we find Gamaliel paralysed with indecision. Here is what he was dealing with. The disciples of Jesus had been filling Jerusalem with their preaching and many thousands had already been converted to Christ. The religious leaders were the ones who had put Jesus to death, and they knew the continued success of the disciples would turn the people against them. At first they were content simply to command that the disciples were not to preach any more (Acts 4:18), but that had only inspired them to even more fervent efforts. With that tactic having failed, many of the Sanhedrin members were convinced that the only way to stop the disciples was to kill them (Acts 5:33).

At this point, Gamaliel spoke up. He and the others had two options, or propositions, on their hands. One was that Jesus Christ was exactly who the disciples declared him to be — the eternal God in human flesh, the God-man. The other was that Jesus Christ was nothing more than a fraud, an impostor who was carrying out a clever ruse.

If the first proposition was true, the only logical course of action for these men was to rethink their position, accept Christ as their Lord and Saviour and encourage the disciples to continue their preaching. If the second proposition was true, their only proper course was to do as some were suggesting — namely, put a stop to the preaching of the disciples. The two propositions could not both be true. The one cancelled out the other.

Gamaliel's counsel

So what did Gamaliel counsel his cohorts? He advised that they embrace both propositions! On the one hand, he suggested they do nothing to stop the preaching of the disciples, but, on the other hand, he made it clear that he did not accept their message. As far as he was concerned, Jesus was not the Son of God, but rather just another in a long line of leaders of political uprisings (Acts 5:36-37).

While others were caught up in the white-hot fever of supporting Christ or opposing him, Gamaliel calmly and deliberately counselled indecision. So carefully chosen and so calmly presented were his words that his argument carried the day. And to this day many are enamoured with Gamaliel's argument, finding in it a logic that is seemingly irrefutable. They drift off, as it were, into a peaceful slumber with the gentle words of Gamaliel sounding sweetly in their ears: 'You can have it both ways. Don't be for Christ, but don't be against him. You can't lose!' But I say to you Gamaliel's logic is the logic of hell! Heed it and you will lose everything!

He ignored the evidence for Christ

I say that for two reasons. First, it ignored the sufficiency of evidence for Christ's claims.

Gamaliel proceeded on the basis that there was not enough evidence to make an intelligent decision about Christ, but that was a totally mistaken assumption. The truth is that there was, and there continues to be, more than enough evidence to substantiate Christ's claims.

When the disciples were hauled before the Sanhedrin to explain why they were still preaching, Simon Peter was quick to present two of the major evidences for Jesus.

The resurrection. The first was his resurrection. Peter said, 'The God of our fathers raised up Jesus whom you murdered by hanging on a tree' (Acts 5:30).

The proofs of the resurrection were so many and so varied that the event could not be denied. If the resurrection had been a farce, we can rest assured the members of the Sanhedrin would have been quick to counter with proofs of their own. But the resurrection was so firmly established that these men had nothing to say by way of rebuttal. Instead, to use the words of an earlier chapter, they were 'cut to the heart' (Acts 2:37).

The transforming power of the Spirit. The second piece of evidence Peter used to support Jesus' claims was the transforming power of the Holy Spirit. He went on: 'And we are his witnesses to these things, and so also is the Holy Spirit whom God has given to those who obey him' (Acts 5:32).

I am sure we fail to appreciate the transformation these men had undergone. A few weeks prior to this they were nothing more than a bunch of whimpering cowards, but here we find them as bold witnesses. How are we to account for such a dramatic transformation? There can only be one answer: they had been changed by the Holy Spirit of God.

If Gamaliel had given serious consideration to just these two evidences, the resurrection of Jesus and the transformation of these disciples, he would have seen how foolhardy it was to advise waiting for more evidence. If this evidence was insufficient, what, we may ask, would Gamaliel have wanted to see? What more was necessary to convince him? The same question must be addressed to all who have followed in Gamaliel's footsteps. God has given more than enough evidence. If you cannot decide about Christ in the face of this evidence, what will it take for you to do so?

He failed to see the impossibility of neutrality

Gamaliel's logic is the logic of hell, then, because he refused to come to grips with the evidence for Christ's claim. But it also is the logic of hell because he failed to see the impossibility of neutrality about Jesus Christ.

Neutrality sounds attractive, but it is a figment of the imagination. Those who profess to be neutral about Christ have already decided against him. By choosing to do nothing with him they do something. Gamaliel called the other members of the Sanhedrin to do nothing about Christ, but the fact is that they had already decided about Christ. They decided when they crucified him a few weeks before. They had stood along with the howling mob that shouted 'Crucify him!' and 'His blood be on us and on our children' (Matt. 27:23-25).

But having made their decision they, by following Gamaliel's advice, chose to act as if they had not decided. They professed to be shocked at the apostles' preaching and, ironically, accused them of trying to bring Christ's blood upon them (Acts 5:28).

Further proof that they had already decided against Christ is seen in their beating of the apostles before they released them (v. 40). A fine piece of neutrality this was! With neutrality like this who needs opposition? Perhaps these men had convinced themselves they were neutral, but they surely would have had great difficulty convincing anyone else.

Our response to the claims of Christ

We grievously err if we fail to ask how Gamaliel's counsel applies to us. The issue he and his friends dealt with that day has come down through the corridors of time and dropped into our laps. The claims of Jesus have never been revoked or withdrawn. The testimony of the disciples reaches from that distant day to say to us that this Jesus Christ is the God-man who arose from the dead and gloriously transforms lives. And we must understand that the law of contradiction still comes into play in the biblical teachings about Jesus Christ. In other words, he cannot be both what the Bible claims he is and not what it claims. He has to be one or the other. There is no middle ground here. Either he is the God-man, or he is not. If he is what the Bible says, he is worthy of our total commitment. If he is not, he is worthy of rejection and even disdain.

What is your response to these claims? Do you hear Gamaliel whispering in your ear as you ponder that question? Do you fancy that you can embrace both sides of the contradiction, that you can both believe in Christ and not believe in him?

If so, you are on the high road to destruction. There are some issues that we simply cannot afford to be neutral about! If a man is told he has a terminal illness and decides to do nothing about it, he has decided to let that illness bring his body to wrack and ruin. Jesus Christ himself spoke plainly of the impossibility of neutrality: 'He who is not with me is against me; and he who does not gather with me scatters abroad' (Matt. 12:30).

The Bible teaches that there is only one way of salvation, and this is through consciously and deliberately trusting in the finished work of Jesus Christ. If you refuse to do that, you will never be saved. You may plead your neutrality until you have exhausted your last breath, but neutrality about Christ cannot save you, because it does not exist. Only by believing in Jesus Christ will you be saved. The words of the apostle John put the issue clearly and squarely before us: 'He who believes in the Son has everlasting life; and he who does not believe the Son shall not see life, but the wrath of God abides on him' (John 3:36).

11.
Festus: the folly of
a casual attitude to crucial truth

Acts 25:13-20

Festus, the Roman governor of Judea, was casual at a time when it was not easy to be. His world was churning and boiling with the ferment of revolution and buffeted with the winds of change. Most men were caught up in the fever of deciding the white-hot controversies of the day, but Festus emerges from the pages of Scripture as one who was content to coast nonchalantly along.

The apostle Paul forced Festus to reveal his colours. Paul had been arrested in Jerusalem for stirring up strife. A plot was hatched by the Jewish leaders to eliminate him before his case could be settled in court (Acts 23:12-14). When word of the plot leaked out Paul was whisked away to Caesarea (Acts 23:23-24). His case was heard by Festus' predecessor, Felix, but the latter simply left Paul for Festus to deal with (Acts 24:27).

Festus heard the charges against Paul and decided to send Paul on to Rome for trial (Acts 25:12). Then King Agrippa arrived for a visit (v. 13). As something of a diversion, it seems, Festus decided to let Paul appear before Agrippa (vv. 14-22).

The interesting thing in all of this is what Festus said in explaining to Agrippa the charges brought against Paul by the Jews: 'They simply had some points of disagreement with him about their own religion and about a certain dead man, Jesus, whom Paul asserted to be alive. And being at a loss how to investigate such matters, I asked whether he was willing to go to Jerusalem and there stand trial on these matters' (vv. 19-20, NASB).

How casually these words dropped from Festus' lips! How lightly his tongue tripped over them! As we read them we wish we could reach down through the long corridor of time, lay hands on him, shake him and say, 'Festus, think about what you just said!'

The significance of the debate about Jesus

What was there for Festus to think about? Simply this — the significance of the point of disagreement between Paul and the Jewish leaders. Give Festus credit for stating it accurately. Paul was indeed insisting that a certain man, Jesus, was alive, and the Jewish leaders were insisting that he was dead.

We are used to hearing and reading about famous people who, although reportedly dead, are said to have been sighted. Adolf Hitler, John F. Kennedy, Elvis Presley and many others are credited with concocting very elaborate schemes to hood-wink the public into thinking they were dead, only to surface in some quiet hamlet. But the issue between Paul and the Jewish leaders was not whether Jesus had actually died. They were all agreed on that. The issue was whether he was still dead or had risen from the grave.

What made the dispute of Paul and the Jewish leaders so vital? Dead men do not just rise from their graves! And if it can be conclusively demonstrated that one has risen, we are faced with two tremendous implications: first, this man is no ordinary man, but is God himself; secondly, if he is God, he is certainly worthy of our worship and obedience.

If you had been at Festus' side when he uttered his casual words, would you not have been tempted to tug at his sleeve and say, 'Think about it, man! If it is true that Jesus arose from the grave as Paul alleges, everything is changed, and we cannot go on living as if it had never happened'?

Festus was face to face with a claim of monumental significance and he waved it aside as though it were nothing. To him it was just a matter of some Jews fussing over their own religion. It never occurred to him that this was not just a matter that concerned the Jews only. If a man had indeed risen from the grave, it quite obviously was far more than a matter of the Jews and their religion. If only Jews had been dying, Festus could have legitimately dismissed the resurrection as something that had significance only for them. But the fact that all those around him were dying and he himself was facing death means the resurrection of Jesus had implications for all.

A lot of people have more or less the same approach as Festus to any claim of spiritual truth. They think it applies only to those who have some natural inclination towards religion. They argue that some people are religious by nature and it is, therefore, acceptable for them to busy themselves with such matters. But those who are not so constituted should be left alone. These people, like Festus, fail to realize that if Jesus arose from the grave it has implications for them as well, religiously inclined or not.

The ease of investigation

It also never occurred to Festus that this was something that could quite easily be investigated and determined. It was not a matter of great complexity that required the work of an expert or genius. Jesus was either dead or alive. This was not an issue that lent itself to ambiguity or neutrality.

When Paul appeared before Agrippa, he said, referring to the resurrection of Jesus, 'This thing was not done in a corner' (Acts 26:26). What did he mean? Anyone who wanted to know whether Jesus was alive could discover the truth easily enough! An event of this magnitude does not take place without creating quite a stir, especially when the dead man appears to various ones around the city! And it was no mere handful of people who saw the Lord Jesus after he arose. Paul assured the Christians in Corinth that over five hundred people had seen the risen Lord at one time (1 Cor. 15:6).

And yet Festus lamely confessed to Agrippa that he was 'at a loss' how to investigate this matter. A trip down to Jerusalem to see the empty tomb and some interviews with those who claimed to have seen the Lord would have gone a long way towards resolving the matter. Festus' problem was not that he had no idea how to investigate this matter, but rather that he did not care enough to make the effort.

With so much at stake one would think no one would be foolish enough to reject Christianity without first investigating it, but the sad fact is that millions are doing exactly that. They reject it, not because they have conducted a diligent investigation and proved it not to be true, but rather because they merely assume it is untrue without having made any effort at all to investigate it.

Section II
Pictures of empty profession

We have looked at some of the men in the Bible who decisively rejected God's way of salvation. Given the opportunity
to break with their sins and cast themselves entirely on Christ,
they turned away and were lost for ever. What tragic figures
these are!

As we look further in the pages of Scripture we note that
there is another class of tragedies: those who seemed to truly
accept Christ but in reality failed to do so.

Few themes are more emphasized and stressed in Scripture
than this. The Lord Jesus included these sober words in his
Sermon on the Mount: 'Not everyone who says to me, "Lord,
Lord," shall enter the kingdom of heaven, but he who does the
will of my Father in heaven. Many will say to me in that day,
"Lord, Lord, have we not prophesied in your name, cast out
demons in your name, and done many wonders in your name?"
And then I will declare to them, "I never knew you; depart
from me, you who practise lawlessness!" ' (Matt. 7:21-23).

These are not the only words Jesus spoke about this matter. His parable of the sower presents four responses to the
gospel, only one of which constituted true acceptance (Matt.
13:23). Another response was the categorical rejection that
we noted in the previous section (Matt. 13:19). The other responses solemnly reflect the reality with which we are dealing.

One of these might be called the response of *emotional acceptance* (Matt. 13:20-21). The hearer, perhaps caught up with the beauty of the music, the size of the congregation, or the eloquence of the preacher, immediately and joyfully scoops up the gospel seed. But when the emotion fades, this type of hearer fades right along with it. A good example of this can be found when Jesus rode into Jerusalem the Sunday before he was crucified. The people, caught in a fever-pitch of excitement, lined the road and cried 'Hosanna' (Matt. 21:9; Mark 11:9-10; John 12:13) as Jesus rode along. In all likelihood, some of those very same people stood beneath Pilate's balcony and cried 'Crucify him!' later that same week (John 19:15).

Another response Jesus highlighted in his parable might be called the response of *partial acceptance*. In this case, the seed of the gospel is choked out by thorns (Matt. 13:22). This is the person who professes faith in the gospel but never really renounces his idols and breaks with his sins. He 'accepts' the Lord, but the primary place in his heart is reserved for the things of this world.

Jesus followed the parable of the sower with the parable of the tares and wheat (Matt. 13:24-30). The tares so closely resemble the wheat that they can hardly be distinguished from it.

Still later, he told the parable of the ten virgins (Matt. 25:1-13). While these virgins appeared to be identical in every way, there was a crucial difference. The five wise virgins had oil in their lamps, while the foolish did not. Similarly, those who have only an empty profession of faith in Christ can look very much like genuine Christians without possessing that thing that makes a Christian, the true knowledge of Christ through the regenerating work of the Holy Spirit of God.

The examples quoted above constitute a mere sample of the emphasis the Lord Jesus gave to this grave issue of empty profession. His apostles emphasized it as well. Paul offered this warning to the Corinthians: 'Examine yourselves as to whether you are in the faith. Test yourselves. Do you not know yourselves, that Jesus Christ is in you? — unless indeed you are disqualified' (2 Cor. 13:5).

It is doubtful whether any theme requires more emphasis today. Public opinion polls unfailingly show that a great percentage of people profess to have had their sins forgiven and to be on their way to heaven. But, alas, their lives do not measure up to their profession. They have little interest in the things of God. The commandments of God exert no influence over the way they live. The worship of God has no appeal to them. Spiritual concerns are regularly pushed to one side in favour of other things.

How are we to explain these things? Some do not hesitate to suggest that all such people are truly saved, but the church has failed to properly disciple them and, therefore, they live as if they are not saved. Others argue that such people are truly saved, but they have not been filled with the Spirit and, therefore, live out their days as 'carnal Christians'. The possibility of professing Christ without truly possessing him seems seldom to come to mind.

One of the ways Scripture combats the tendency to ignore this possibility is by holding before us some tragic instances of men who made an empty profession. In this section we focus on three of these.

12.
The wedding guest: a faulty acceptance of the gospel invitation

Matthew 22:1-14

This parable brings us face to face with the dreadful, horrifying possibility of missing out on the kingdom of God, or, to put it another way, falling short of the kingdom of God.

There is more than one way to fall short of the kingdom. One way is through categorical rejection. This possibility is set out in the first seven verses of this parable. Most of the Jews of Jesus' time fell into this category. The apostle John bluntly states their rejection of Jesus in these words: 'He came to his own, and his own did not receive him' (John 1:11).

During the last week of his earthly life, Jesus gave the Jewish leaders one last warning about the danger of rejecting him and missing out on his kingdom. He told three parables in quick succession, parables of rejection. The first pictured their rejection in terms of a son rebelling against his father (Matt. 21:28-32); the second as tenants rebelling against their landlord (Matt. 21:33-44); and the third, the parable we are considering in this chapter, in terms of subjects rebelling against their rightful king.

This parable goes beyond merely presenting the rejection of Christ. It actually foretells in a very graphic way what was going to happen as a result of this rejection. For one thing, the Jewish nation would experience terrible judgement. Thirty-seven short years after they crucified Jesus, the Jews saw the

Romans devastate the city of Jerusalem and their temple. Perhaps some of those who witnessed that recalled the words of this parable: 'And he sent out his armies, destroyed those murderers, and burned up their city' (Matt. 22:7).

A second result of the Jewish nation's rejection of Jesus was that the gospel would be carried to the Gentiles. This is pictured in the second half of this parable (vv. 8-14). The parable falls quite naturally, then, into two parts. The first part deals with the Jews' rejection of Christ (vv. 1-7), and the second part deals with the gospel going to the Gentiles (vv. 8-14). It is this second half of the parable that presents us with a very serious danger indeed, that of a faulty acceptance of the gospel.

The elements of the parable

This danger is presented to us in terms of a man who accepted the king's invitation to the wedding feast he was holding in honour of his son. The following elements stand out with crystal clarity: an invitation, a condition attached to the invitation, an inspection and an indictment.

An invitation with a condition attached

The invitation goes out to all (vv. 9-10), and along with it is the announcement that all who attend must wear a proper wedding garment. There would be no difficulty at this point because the king himself would provide the garment.

How do we know that this condition went out with the invitation? The parable tells us that the wedding guest in question was 'speechless' when he was confronted with his failure to wear the garment (v. 12). He could not plead ignorance because he had been told. He could not plead that he did not have a proper garment to wear because the king himself had promised to provide the garment.

An inspection

This confrontation came about because the king conducted an inspection of his guests (v. 11). He was not content merely to invite guests to his wedding feast and to ask that they wear the garment he provided. He actually walked among them to see if they had complied.

An indictment

The refusal of this one guest to wear the garment resulted in the king pronouncing this fearful sentence: 'Bind him hand and foot, take him away, and cast him into outer darkness; there will be weeping and gnashing of teeth' (v. 13).

The elements of the gospel

Jesus' parables were not just entertaining stories. They drew upon familiar things in order to drive home spiritual truth. The elements of this parable are present in the gospel of Jesus Christ.

There is an invitation in the gospel. What a glorious invitation it is! It is the invitation to all to come and share in that joyous time when the Lord Jesus Christ himself will take his bride, the church, home to himself in heaven. There will be at that time a wedding feast such as has never been known before (Rev. 19:1-9).

But along with this invitation a condition is announced: all who accept the invitation must be clothed in the proper wedding garment. There can be no doubt about the nature of this garment. It is the garment of perfect righteousness. The Bible affirms that God is a holy God (Isa. 6:3; Rev. 4:8) and heaven is a holy place (Rev. 21:27). If we are to enter into this holy place and enjoy fellowship with this holy God, we must be holy ourselves.

Now here is a piercing dilemma: God demands perfect holiness of us, and we have nothing to offer but sin. How then can we ever hope to stand in the presence of God? The happy news of the gospel is that God himself has provided the garment of perfect righteousness we need. He has done it in and through his Son, Jesus Christ. Jesus took our humanity unto himself and lived a life of perfect righteousness. While we have broken God's laws time without number, he did not break a single one. Having lived that life of perfect righteousness, he went to the cross to suffer in his own person the penalty of God upon sin. He did everything necessary for guilty sinners to stand before God in heaven. God demands perfect righteousness; we have nothing but sin. But Jesus paid for the sins of all who believe and offers them his righteousness. The sins of his people were put on his account and his righteousness was put on theirs.

The whole problem with the wedding guest in Jesus' parable can be put in this way: he accepted the invitation without accepting the condition. His error has been constantly repeated throughout history and continues to be to this very hour. The gospel invitation goes out to be part of God's great wedding feast, and many say, 'Yes, I believe in God and in heaven, and I want to be with him in heaven when I die.' But when the gospel proceeds to announce that God requires the garment of perfect righteousness that is available only through his Son, they, as it were, casually brush off their own tattered garment and say, 'This will be good enough.'

But it will not be good enough. The same Bible which tells us about the perfect righteousness God demands, the terrible reality of our sins and the finished work of the Lord Jesus

Christ, also tells us that there is a great inspection day coming. No one will slip into heaven incognito. No one will be standing there in the rags of his own righteousness and not be seen. No one without the garment of Christ's righteousness will escape detection.

Those who are without the righteousness of Christ will be without excuse on that day, and they will hear the same terrifying sentence that the wedding guest heard: 'Bind him hand and foot, take him away, and cast him into outer darkness; there will be weeping and gnashing of teeth' (Matt. 22:13).

The wedding guest in Jesus' parable stands as a warning to all of us about the possibility of a faulty acceptance of the gospel, and a faulty acceptance is no better than outright rejection.

13.
Judas Iscariot: a warning against apostasy

John 13:21-30; 18:1-3

If ever a man appeared to be eternally safe, it was Judas Iscariot. Jesus' choice of him as one of his twelve disciples would seem to mean he had been graciously visited by the Spirit of God and removed from the possibility of being lost eternally.

Even if we allow that Judas was unconverted at the time he was chosen by Jesus, we find ourselves inclined to believe it would have been impossible for him to remain so. No man has ever enjoyed greater privileges, or moved in a realm more likely to lead one to the knowledge of the truth. Enormous spiritual privileges doggedly and continually pursued Judas each day for a wonderful stretch of more than three years.

What Judas heard

During those years Judas heard the teaching of Jesus. Others gave testimony to the unparalleled and unprecedented nature of that teaching. Matthew's Gospel reports that his hearers were 'astonished' at his teaching, 'for he taught them as one having authority, and not as the scribes' (Matt. 7:28-29). When Jesus taught in the synagogue of Nazareth, his hearers 'marvelled at the gracious words which proceeded out of his mouth' (Luke 4:22). Even officers dispatched by the Sanhedrin court returned to say, 'No man ever spoke like this man!' (John 7:46).

Judas Iscariot heard those teachings that amazed and moved so many. He heard the matchless Sermon on the Mount and its chilling warning about being deceived (Matt. 7:21-23). He heard Jesus plainly tell his hearers of judgement to come and the need to repent and place their trust in him (e.g. Luke 13:1-5), but while others trembled and repented, Judas did not.

When a multitude became offended at the teaching of Jesus and ceased following him, Simon Peter stayed with him because he heard in those same teachings the authentic ring of eternal life (John 6:68). Judas Iscariot heard those same words and, while he also stayed with Jesus, it was not because of those words.

What Judas saw

Keeping pace with the glory of what Judas heard is what he saw. No man has seen more! Lame men walking, blind men seeing, deaf men hearing — all as a result of the mighty power of Jesus and all, so far as we know, witnessed by Judas Iscariot.

On three occasions, Jesus prised open the jaws of death and released its prey. And on each occasion Judas saw, if not the act itself, at least the results of it (Mark 5:37-43; Luke 7.11-17; John 11:43-44).

He was on the scene when Jesus took meagre fare and fed multitudes (Matt. 14:15-21; 15:32-38). He saw Jesus still storms (Mark 4:35-39) and cast out demons (Mark 1:32-34; 5:1-15). He had even been able to perform miracles himself in the name of the Lord Jesus (Matt. 10:1,4).

Judas Iscariot was present when Mary of Bethany, melted by love for Christ, poured out her costly ointment on the feet of Christ and wiped them with her hair. But while Mary's heart

was speaking freely of her love for the Lord, Judas was pee-
vishly complaining about the waste of the ointment (John
12:1-8).

Perhaps the most touching of all, Judas, on the night before
Jesus was crucified, saw the Lord kneel before him and tenderly wash his feet (John 13:1-5). That wondrous act of con-
descension and service was followed by Jesus' plain intimation
to Judas that he was fully aware of what Judas was about to
do (John 13:26-27).

But nothing stopped Judas. He left the room immediately
after Jesus spoke to him, and the apostle John, recording the
event years later, summed up Judas' departure with the words:
'And it was night' (John 13:30). Indeed it was. The darkness
of the night was no match for the darkness of Judas' soul.

What Judas did

Later that evening, Judas led a band of men to the Garden of
Gethsemane to arrest Jesus. The darkness of the night made it
essential that someone be able to positively identify Jesus. Judas did so by approaching him with the greeting 'Rabbi, Rabbi!'
and kissing him (Mark 14:45).

Why did Judas do this foul thing? Some suggest that he
had no choice in the matter, that he was predestined to do it
and that he was a mere robot in the hands of God. There can
be no doubt that God's predestination was at work here. Centuries before Judas was ever born, the psalmist David foretold
the event (Ps. 41:9; 55:12-14). But God's predestination com-
prehends the means as well as the end; that is, it embodies the
choices of men. Judas betrayed Jesus because he wanted to do
so.

How could he desire to deliver to death the one with whom
he had been so closely associated, the one from whom he had

heard so many wonderful teachings and whom he had seen perform so many glorious deeds? We do know he was a thief because the apostle John tells us that he dipped into the disciples' treasury from time to time (John 12:6). His interest in material things may very well have caused him to aspire to a position of influence — and the wealth it would bring — in an earthly kingdom set up by Jesus. When it became apparent to him that Jesus had no interest in doing so, he may have become disillusioned.

Some have even suggested that Judas' act of betrayal was designed so to put Jesus into a corner with the authorities that he would have no choice except to use his power to set up his kingdom. The fact that Jesus so clearly taught that his kingdom was not of this world makes this an unlikely scenario.

Whatever course we follow in seeking to explain Judas' action, we must not lose sight of the main thing. S. G. DeGraaf puts it powerfully: 'Judas was an unbeliever! Enthusiastically he had followed Christ as a disciple... Yet, he had closed his heart to what was essential in Christ, to the grace of God in him, and therefore he had not been able or willing to believe in him.'[1]

Some take exception to this. They insist that Judas was a genuine believer in Christ and that his act of betrayal should not be considered to be any worse than Simon Peter's denial of Christ. In other words, they contend that Judas was a believer who sinned, rather than an unbeliever. The Bible, however, gives us no room for doubt on this matter. The Lord Jesus himself referred to Judas as a 'devil' (John 6:70) and 'the son of perdition' (John 17:12). These are not terms that can be applied to the saints of God, even when they falter and fail as Simon Peter did.

Because Judas was content with only an outward show of allegiance to Christ and was not a genuine believer in him and his redemption, he came to a terrible end. Scripture tells us that he went out and hanged himself (Matt. 27:3-10), but that was not his end. Terrible and gruesome as that act was, it could not compare with the hell that yawned to receive his soul. That same fate awaits all those who join Judas in his rejection of Christ (2 Thess. 1:8-10).

A solemn warning

Scripture calls our attention to Judas so that we will take heed to the lesson that he teaches. That lesson may be put in this way: a person can be closely associated with the things of God and still be lost for ever. The author of the epistle to the Hebrews gives a clear warning about this: 'For it is impossible for those who were once enlightened, and have tasted the heavenly gift, and have become partakers of the Holy Spirit, and have tasted the good word of God and the powers of the age to come, if they fall away, to renew them again to repentance, since they crucify again for themselves the Son of God, and put him to an open shame' (Heb. 6:4-6). Each of this author's descriptions can be applied to Judas. He was enlightened. He heard the truth from Jesus and intellectually comprehended it. He tasted of the heavenly gift. He actually witnessed the power of heaven at work. He partook of the Holy Spirit. The Lord Jesus was endued with the Spirit of God, and to the extent that Judas received and appreciated the ministry of Jesus, he partook of that gift. He tasted the good word of God. As we have noted, Judas received the Word of God from the lips of Jesus, and to some extent actually enjoyed it. He tasted the power of the age to come. The signs and wonders performed by Jesus clearly pointed Judas beyond this earthly realm to the heavenly realm. But with it all, Judas was lost.

Each of these expressions can also be applied to us. It is possible for us to understand and appreciate spiritual things, and, like Judas, be lost for ever.

This is all very serious and thought-provoking. But there is also cheering news. While it is possible for a lost person to go so far in religion that he appears to be saved, it is not possible for one who has truly been saved ever to be lost. The saved person may indeed appear to be like an unsaved person, but he will not stay in that position. The saved person can sin, and sin dreadfully, but he will in due time come to his senses and come to repentance. Samuel E. Waldron writes, 'True Christians renew their repentance and faith in Christ (Luke 22:32,61-62; 1 Cor. 11:32). Just as the elect will not die before they are converted, so the regenerate will not die before they repent.'[2]

14.
Simon Magus:
a false view of the gospel

Acts 8:9-24

This passage brings before us a very important person. Simon Magus is not important because he plays a large role in Scripture. His name only appears in this one passage. His importance is due to the fact that he represents a danger that threatens untold multitudes today: the danger of an empty profession of faith in the Lord Jesus Christ.

Simon made his profession when Philip, one of the deacons of the early church (Acts 6:5), came to the city of Samaria to share the gospel of Christ. Philip's preaching met with a tremendous response as 'multitudes' embraced it (Acts 8:6).

Simon Magus himself is said to have believed the message (v. 13). He also publicly identified himself as a follower of Christ through baptism (v. 13). Nor was that all: he so much enjoyed being with Philip that he accompanied him on a regular basis (v. 13).

We may rest assured that no convert in Samaria was more noted than Simon. This man had practised sorcery for a long time (v. 11). Through satanic power he had been able actually to perform astonishing signs. No one would have expected Simon to renounce his sorcery and receive the Lord Jesus Christ, but that is what he did, or appeared to do.

All seemed to be well with Simon for a while. Then Peter and John arrived from the church of Jerusalem (v. 14). The gift of the Holy Spirit had been withheld from the new Samaritan believers until these two apostles arrived. The reason for this is not hard to determine. Jews and Samaritans had long despised each other, and it was essential that this rift should not be carried over into the life of the church. By withholding the Spirit until Peter and John arrived, the Lord was bringing unity between the Jewish and the Samaritan Christians.

It was the ministry of Peter and John that brought the true colours of Simon Magus to light. He was amazed that the gift of the Holy Spirit was bestowed through the action of these apostles in laying their hands on the Samaritan believers. And he was envious. How wonderful it would be if he could only exercise this power! Perhaps Peter and John would share their secret if he offered them a tidy sum of money.

Simon Magus seriously miscalculated. The apostle Peter responded to his offer with these devastating words: 'Your money perish with you, because you thought that the gift of God could be purchased with money! You have neither part nor portion in this matter, for your heart is not right in the sight of God' (vv. 20-21). As if that were not enough, Peter further stated that Simon Magus was 'poisoned by bitterness and bound by iniquity' (v. 23).

Peter's words leave no room for doubt or debate. Although Simon Magus made a profession of faith in Christ, was baptized and associated himself with Philip, he was not truly a child of God. He had been deceived about his true standing with God.

How are we to explain such a thing? How is it possible for an individual to be deceived about this matter of salvation? We can gather some answers from this account of Simon Magus.

A distorted view of the gospel

First, we must say that Simon misconstrued the purpose, or the object, of the gospel.

When Philip arrived in Samaria, he found that Simon had been practising sorcery for a great number of years. Sorcery stems from very practical concerns. It seeks to contact spirits from the realm of the dead. The purpose in doing so is to help the living find answers. It is true, of course, that many of these questions have to do with the future, but the purpose behind them is to make life more comfortable for the living. Sorcery is very much a concern of the here and now.

In addition to that, sorcery had been Simon's ticket to personal aggrandisement and advancement. He had used it to gain notoriety for himself. Before Philip arrived on the scene, the people of Samaria were so astonished by Simon's powers that they went around saying, 'This man is the great power of God' (v. 10).

When Simon offered money to Peter and John, it was evident that his whole view of the gospel was wrong. He had looked upon it as another way to secure the same thing that he had been using his sorcery to achieve, as an exclusively here-and-now proposition. It was just one more choice on the supermarket shelf of ideas for coping with life in this world. To Simon the gospel was a commodity to be used to secure comfort and happiness in this world.

Furthermore, Simon saw the giving of the Holy Spirit as an even better way to gain the notice and applause of his fellow-citizens. It is evident that the arrival of Philip, Peter and John in Samaria had shifted the focus from Simon. He was no longer on centre stage in Samaria, and he yearned to regain the spotlight. We may say, therefore, that Simon looked upon the gospel as a means of getting things.

All of this has a most familiar ring to it. Healing for the

body, money in the pocket, success in business — these are just some of the things that will be ours, we are told, if we will only learn how to practise certain Christian principles, and if we will just have enough faith.

While the Christian faith does, of course, have a wonderfully transforming effect on life in this world, we are never to view it primarily in terms of this world. The gospel of Christ is primarily concerned with our sinful condition. The Bible tells us that we are sinners by nature and, because of that, we are under the just condemnation of God. That sentence of condemnation has already been pronounced (John 3:18), and the wrath of God already hovers like a dark cloud over us (John 3:36). But it will reach its final and fullest expression when we finally come before God's throne of judgement. At that time we shall be separated from him for ever and be cast into what the apostle Paul calls 'everlasting destruction' (2 Thess. 1:8 10).

This is the terrible reality the gospel was designed to deal with. And it deals with it through the redeeming death of the Lord Jesus Christ. There on the cross Jesus endured the wrath of God in the place of sinners. Those who decisively break with their sins and cast themselves on that redeeming death have nothing to fear. Because Jesus took the wrath of God in their stead, there is no wrath left for them. The wrath of God exhausted itself in falling upon Jesus, and all those who trust him are delivered from it for ever.

All of this, of course, brings peace and comfort to us in this life, but that is a far cry from saying peace and comfort in this life are the sole, or even the primary, concerns of the gospel. The truth is that the gospel calls all those who embrace it to bear a cross of their own, the cross of service to the Lord Jesus Christ and suffering for his dear name. Those who think the gospel is to make life in this world easy and comfortable would remove that cross and replace it with a couch.

A spirit that had not been humbled

We can go yet further and say that Simon was deceived because he failed to understand the spirit with which the gospel must be received.

The fact that he offered money to Peter and John indicates that he totally misunderstood the gracious nature of God's dealings with man. The giving of the Holy Spirit through the laying on of hands was not something that Peter and John had earned, or deserved, or purchased. It was something that was given to them by God. By offering money for this gift, Simon was attacking the very heart and soul of Christianity. He approached it as a transaction, essentially saying, 'If I do this, God must in turn do the other.'

Multitudes have 'the Simon mentality'. They come to God jingling their coins in their pocket, ready to make him an offer he cannot refuse. Some come with the coin of good works in their pocket and say, 'If I live a good life, God will have to give me salvation.' Some come with the coin of church membership. Some even come with literal coins, thinking that if they give a substantial amount of money to the church, God will be obligated to save them.

There is no shortage of coins that men are willing to offer God for salvation, but there is also no coin that can purchase salvation. It is the gift of God (Eph. 2:8-9), and there is nothing we can do to earn it or deserve it. Salvation comes, not to those who have their pockets stuffed with various coins, but to those who see their sin and see that they have no power to deal with that sin. It comes to those who cast themselves totally on Christ, and who recognize that even that act of casting themselves on Christ is something they cannot do in and of themselves, but it is something they are enabled to do by the Spirit of God.

Salvation comes to those who truly and wholeheartedly take up these familiar words:

Not the labour of my hands
Can fulfil thy law's demands:
Could my zeal no respite know,
Could my tears for ever flow,
All for sin could not atone;
Thou must save, and thou alone.

Nothing in my hand I bring,
Simply to thy cross I cling:
Naked, come to thee for dress:
Helpless, look to thee for grace...

(Augustus Toplady)

The power of sin was unbroken

Finally, we must say Simon was deceived because the power of sin was never broken in his life. The apostle Peter made this clear when Simon came rattling his coins and offering to buy the gift of the Holy Spirit. Peter responded by saying Simon was 'poisoned by bitterness and bound by iniquity' (Acts 8:23).

That is the tragic nature of sin. It is no small, trifling thing. It is like poison that affects the whole man. It is bondage. Only the power of God can flush out the poison and break the bondage. We cannot do it ourselves. But once God has done this work for us, once he has broken the power of sin in our lives, evidence will show up in our lives. Simon's actions proved he was still in the grip of sin. We often hear these days that it is possible to be truly saved and still live in sin, that our hearts can be cleansed while our conduct is foul. But this is a lie from the devil. Our conduct is an accurate indicator of what is in our hearts (Matt. 12:33-35).

Simon was, therefore, in a very serious condition. He had made a profession of faith, but he was still in his sins. While Peter refused to minimize the seriousness of Simon's condition, he did not regard it as hopeless. If Simon would sincerely repent, the forgiveness that had escaped him would be his (Acts 8:22). The hope Peter extended to Simon is extended to all. Empty profession can give way to true faith in Jesus.

Section III
Pictures of acceptance

The Bible does not shrink from telling us hard truths. It tells us about those who made shipwreck of their lives by refusing to embrace the saving gospel of the Lord Jesus Christ. But while the Bible does not mince words on this matter, it also sounds a much happier note. It presents numerous instances of true conversion. The chapters in this section are intended to give us a mere taste of the many examples of glorious conversions found in Scripture. These examples show that while pitfalls and dangers abound on every hand to keep us from the knowledge of Christ, no one need despair. The grace of God that brings salvation can overcome all these perils.

15.
Naaman: overcoming the temptation to stand on our dignity

2 Kings 5:8-15

Naaman was a great man. He was captain of Syria's army and was admired and respected by all. Wherever he went people fussed over him and bragged about his great military exploits. If Naaman were alive today, he would be a celebrity. He would find it difficult to go out in public without people seeking his autograph, and we would undoubtedly find his picture on the front page of *People* or *Time*. We would find him making appearances on the various talk shows and we would not be surprised to hear of him being selected as the guest of honour at some public function.

Celebrity status does not insulate one from the problems and trials of life, and Naaman had a problem, a very serious problem. He was a leper. Leprosy in that day was the medical equivalent to AIDS today. It was the same thing as hearing one's death sentence read.

Naaman's whole world had come crashing down around him. Military exploits, fame and fortune meant nothing now. He had leprosy, and that meant he was going to die a slow, agonizing death.

But suddenly Naaman found himself the focus of a remarkable chain of events. A little girl he had brought back from Israel as a slave for his wife had an interesting story to tell.

She said there was a prophet in Israel who could heal Naaman of his leprosy. It sounded too good to be true, but Naaman decided to mention it to the King of Syria. The king immediately dispatched Naaman and a letter to the King of Israel. The King of Israel was flabbergasted when he read the letter because it seemed to indicate that Syria's king was expecting him to heal Naaman. The prophet Elisha saved the day by telling the King of Israel to send Naaman to him.

A cure offered and rejected

So the chain of events led Naaman at long last to the house of Elisha, and that is where we find him in the verses cited at the head of this chapter. Naaman did not have to wait long. The prophet soon sent his servant out with this message: 'Go and wash in the Jordan seven times, and your flesh shall be restored to you, and you shall be clean' (v. 10).

Just think for a moment about what is happening in this scene. Here is Naaman with the most dreaded disease of his time, a disease for which there was absolutely no cure apart from divine intervention. And here, on the other hand, is the prophet telling him that God would intervene on his behalf if he would simply go down to the Jordan river and wash seven times. What would you have done if you had been in Naaman's shoes? Wouldn't you have thanked the servant of Elisha for delivering the message, asked him to thank Elisha and his God for the cure and headed towards the Jordan? That was not Naaman's reaction. Instead of graciously thanking Elisha and hastening to the Jordan, he threw a tantrum! He flew into a rage! Can you imagine it? A terminally ill man is told of a cure that is available for his illness, and he is enraged by it and turns away. How silly and childish!

The reason for the rejection

What possessed Naaman to do such a thing? We have no need to search long for the answer to that question. Naaman gives it to us. In the Authorized Version, it is all wrapped up in those two little words: 'I thought...' (2 Kings 5:11). The New King James Version uses four words to translate it: 'I said to myself...'

In other words, Naaman came to Elisha's house with certain preconceptions in his mind. He had it all figured out ahead of time. He had in his own mind, and with his own wisdom, determined exactly how Elisha should go about this business of effecting the cure. It was not enough for him to have his leprosy cured; he wanted it cured in a way that accommodated his preconceptions and his own wisdom. When Elisha's servant came out and announced what he must do, Naaman's wisdom was violated and his preconceptions were shattered.

What snippet of advice did his wisdom whisper into his ear as he rode to Elisha's house? What was it that Naaman was thinking when he came to Elisha's door? It was that any cure Elisha proposed should take into account his dignity and his standing. In other words, as Alexander Maclaren points out, Naaman wanted to be treated like a great man who happened to be a leper, but Elisha's cure treated him as a leper who happened to be a great man.[1]

The cure Elisha proposed not only ignored Naaman's greatness; it also went out of its way to humble him. First, Elisha did not even extend to him the courtesy of going out to meet him (v. 11). Elisha was not interested in his greatness and did not want his autograph.

Secondly, Elisha's cure completely ignored the fact that Naaman had brought an enormous fortune with him to pay for the cure (v. 5). The cure was the result of God's grace and there was, therefore, no place for Naaman's gold, silver or clothing.

Thirdly, the cure required him to do something that he personally found to be undesirable and repulsive — namely, to bathe in the waters of the Jordan (v. 12). This offended Naaman on two grounds. First, the Jordan was a muddy, filthy river, and he did not think it fitting for one of his standing to have to stoop so low as to bathe in such waters. On top of that, it violated Naaman's national pride. To his way of thinking, if the cure was just a matter of bathing in a river, the rivers of his own country, Syria, would be far better than any river in Israel.

Besides, this bathing was something that any child could do. Naaman had come prepared to do 'something great' (v. 13), and the prophet asked him to do something simple.

The error of Naaman repeated

What does all this have to do with us? The sober truth is that there are multitudes who are doing exactly the same as Naaman. You see, the Bible tells us we are all afflicted with the dreadful, deadly disease of sin — a disease which is even more deadly than Naaman's leprosy because it ultimately issues in eternal destruction. The Bible also tells us there is absolutely no cure for sin except through divine intervention. But, wonder of wonders, the Bible also says God has intervened and made a cure available in and through the person of his Son, Jesus Christ. This Christ, by his perfect life and his atoning death, has done all that is necessary for our sins to be forgiven and for us to have eternal life in heaven.

Isn't that incredibly glorious good news? A cure is available for our sins! One would think the overwhelming majority would fall over themselves to embrace the gospel cure and assure themselves of eternity in heaven, but, amazingly enough, there are multitudes who do as Naaman did. After hearing the good news of a cure, they turn away. It is not that they do not need a cure for sin. They do! And it is not that a cure is not available. It is!

Why, then, do so many turn away from the cure? The answer is that the gospel offends them. It violates their wisdom and their sense of dignity. It does not take into account their riches, social standing, or education. It says all without exception are in sin, and it also says there is absolutely nothing we can do to earn or deserve salvation, but we are entirely dependent on the grace of God. We want to come before God with Naaman's shekels and changes of clothing, and have him accept us on the basis of who we are and what we have done. But just as Elisha ignored Naaman's wealth and dignity, so God refuses all our attempts to stand before him on the basis of our own merits or accomplishments.

Furthermore, the gospel requires that we do something that seems ludicrous and even repugnant. It tells us we must bow in repentance and faith before Jesus' atoning death on the cross. This offends many. They look at that bloody cross and they find themselves thinking there must be another way, a way that is more sophisticated and appealing. They, like Naaman, have no trouble thinking of other things that make more sense, but the finger of God points unrelentingly at that cross as the one and only way of salvation.

No generation has been more impressed with human wisdom and dignity than our own. Our age is absorbed with human rights, equality and fairness. This is not to say there is not a legitimate place for these concerns. We are all made in the image of God, and this does indeed give every human being a basic dignity and provides the basis for human rights.

But the proper place for emphasizing human dignity is in our relationship to others, not in our relationship to God. Human dignity is fine among human beings but it is insufficient when it comes to standing before the Lord. Our dignity comes from God, but we must never use it as an excuse for not bowing before him. Many have trouble making this distinction, and when the gospel confronts them with its demand for submission, the spirit of Naaman can easily come to life in them.

The acquiescence of Naaman

But let's get back to Naaman. Fortunately, his servants saw that he was foolishly turning away from the only hope he had for a cure and they began to reason with him. Their reasoning was so simple. If Elisha had asked him to perform some extraordinary feat, he would not have hesitated to attempt it. Why then was he baulking at doing something so simple?

At last Naaman saw his folly and agreed to go to the Jordan. There he completely obeyed the word of the Lord through Elisha, and immediately after his seventh washing his flesh was 'restored like the flesh of a little child' (v. 14).

What did Naaman do when he saw his flesh? Did he leap for joy? Did he hug all his servants? Did he kiss the horses pulling his chariot? The Bible does not say. One thing it does say is that he made his way back to Elisha's house. How different things were on this second visit! This time the prophet did see him. And this time Naaman has different words on his lips. Instead of saying, 'I thought…' he is able to say, 'I know…' He says, 'Indeed, now I know that there is no God in all the earth, except in Israel…' (v. 15).

What a great lesson there is here! If we ever want to be able to say 'I know…' we must stop saying, 'I thought…' In other words, if we ever want to have the joy and the peace and the confidence the gospel brings, we must stop arguing with God and accept the gospel as the only cure for sin. We must stop standing on our dignity and our wisdom and bow before the wisdom of God in Christ Jesus.

16.
Nathanael: overcoming prejudices against the truth

John 1:43-51

If you could meet anyone from the past, whom would you choose? It seems a very foolish question. These people have passed from the stage of human history and there is no way we can meet them in this life.

Yet there is a sense in which that is not true. We can still meet these people. They still live on the written page, written either by themselves or someone else. One of the most fascinating and rewarding dimensions of Bible study is this: it brings to life men and women who lived thousands of years ago. Through the pages of the Bible we can in a sense meet these people and learn from them.

We are, of course, familiar with the great names of the Bible: Abraham, Moses, David, Isaiah and Paul. There can be no doubt about the importance of meeting these men in the pages of Scripture. But there are also lesser-known figures who have vital and powerful lessons to teach us.

Consider Nathanael. If any one of us were to be asked to start naming Bible characters, it would no doubt take us a long time to get around to Nathanael. His name does not exactly spring to our minds when we think of Bible characters. But Nathanael, one of the original twelve disciples of Jesus, is a man everyone should meet.

A message that still applies

Why is it important to meet Nathanael? The first reason is that he received a message that still applies.

One day as he was sitting under a fig tree, his friend Philip suddenly burst upon him with these words: 'We have found him of whom Moses in the law, and also the prophets, wrote — Jesus of Nazareth, the son of Joseph' (John 1:45).

This was no small claim. When sin came into the human race through Adam and Eve, God announced that he would send a Saviour. The entire Old Testament anticipates the coming of that Saviour. The law of Moses held before people the demands of a holy God and their complete inability to meet those demands and, in so doing, pointed them to their need for the coming Saviour who would meet all those demands.

The sacrificing of animals held before the people the nature of what this Saviour would do. Because of the guilt of their sin, the people themselves deserved to die, but those animals were put to death in their stead. Those animals could not, of course, actually take the place of human beings and pay the penalty for their sins, but they could and did point ahead to the Saviour who could in reality take the place of sinners and bear in his own person the penalty of eternal death.

The preaching of the prophets held before the people that same coming Saviour and his redeeming death on behalf of sinners (Isa. 53).

Some see the Old Testament era as a time when God was first trying one plan of salvation and then another, but God has always had only one way of salvation, and that way was, and is, his Son, Jesus Christ. The people of the Old Testament were saved in exactly the same way as we are today — that is, through faith in Christ. The only difference is that they looked forward in faith to the coming of Christ, while we look backward in faith to his coming.

What Philip announced to Nathanael on this occasion was, then, truly staggering and monumental. Generation after generation had come and gone, and God's promised Saviour had not come. But now Philip was standing before Nathanael saying, 'We have found him!'

The happy message Philip announced on this occasion has not been withdrawn. It was good news on that day, and it is still good news today. The Christ whom Philip found came to provide eternal salvation by dying on the cross, and that salvation is still available today.

A mind-set that still exists

The second reason we should meet Nathanael is because he reflected a mind-set that still exists. We would like to think that Nathanael responded to Philip's news by leaping to his feet and joyfully shouting: 'Show me the way!' But he did not. The news Philip announced must have sounded like a beautiful melody in his ears until he got to that part about Nazareth. That word interrupted the melody with a dreadful clang.

Perhaps Nathanael was thinking of the prophecy of Micah about the Messiah being born in Bethlehem (Micah 5: 2). Perhaps he assumed the glorious Messiah could not possibly come from a town as unappealing and undistinguished as Nazareth. Whatever flashed through his mind, it was sufficient for him to conclude that Philip was mistaken. This Jesus might be very wonderful and special, but he could not be the Messiah. The thing was simply inconceivable. Nathaniel could not at this point accept the message because he had a preconceived notion that ruled it out.

Nathaniel was not the last to have a predisposition against the truth. Let someone proclaim the good news that forgiveness of sins and eternal life in heaven are available in Christ and many, because of their bias against the truth, will rule it out before even listening to the evidence. They say, 'Eternal salvation through a Jewish rabbi dying on a Roman cross two thousand years ago? The thing is ridiculous. It is simply inconceivable. No one in his right mind would believe such a message.'

To those who are in the grip of a bias against the truth, we Christians take up the words of Philip to Nathanael: 'Come and see' (John 1:46). We ask you to suspend your bias long enough to come and take a hard look at the evidence for Christ.

Evidence that must still be considered

This brings us to yet another reason why we should meet Nathanael: he encountered evidence he could not deny. Philip's invitation was one Nathanael could not resist. Even if Jesus could not be the Messiah, it was obvious that he had made such an impression on Philip that Nathanael had to learn more about him. Scripture does not tell us what Nathanael expected to find when he encountered Jesus. His grand assumption about Nazareth certainly ruled out any expectation of finding the Messiah. But that is exactly what he found.

As he and Philip approached, Jesus said to him, 'Behold, an Israelite indeed, in whom is no deceit!' (v. 47).

Nathanael's response was just what we would expect. He was a sceptical sort of person who would not jump to conclusions without evidence, and he could not, therefore, accept Jesus' commendation without knowing how he had arrived at it. 'How do you know me?', he asked (v. 48).

Jesus' answer not only caught Nathanael off guard but also changed him for ever: 'Before Philip called you, when you were under the fig tree, I saw you' (v. 48).

Jesus' assessment of Nathanael was not just a lucky guess or unsubstantiated flattery designed to curry favour. It was based on personal knowledge. That knowledge was so extensive and penetrating that it even extended to the cover of a fig tree. There Nathanael could be hidden from the eyes of others, but he was not hidden from the Christ.

Nathanael's bias melted in the bright glare of Jesus' omniscience. Nathanael now knew the truth about Jesus, and he quickly and powerfully confessed that truth: 'Rabbi, you are the Son of God! You are the King of Israel!' (v. 49).

It is interesting that Nathanael had nothing to say about Nazareth. He still did not know how Nazareth fitted into this puzzle, but he could not allow what he did not know to obscure what he did know. This Jesus was the Messiah. There could be no other explanation for him. Nathanael could wait to find out about Nazareth, but he could not wait to confess the faith that flooded into his heart. Christians do not believe in Christ because he has given them the answer to every single question that has ever cropped up in their minds but rather because they have encountered overwhelming evidence that he is indeed God in human flesh.

The Gospel accounts of his penetrating insight into men, such as we have here with Nathanael, are only one such evidence (John 2:23-25; 4:17-19,29). We also have those passages that explicitly affirm that Jesus knew what lay ahead of him (Matt. 16:21; 17:22-23; 20:17-19). Then there are those episodes in which he demonstrated his power over disease (Matt. 4:23-24; 9:35; 14:34-36; Mark 1:34), nature (Mark 4:35-39) and death itself (Mark 5:35-43; Luke 7:11-15; John 11:43-44).

In addition to these we find numerous passages which demonstrate his fulfilment in minute detail of the centuries-old prophecies of the Old Testament (e.g. Matt. 21:5,9; 27:35;

see also Luke 24:27,44). The icing on the cake, so to speak, is
his own resurrection from the dead.

Armed with such evidence, the Christian knows he can
confidently wait to have his lesser questions answered. Once
one has had the big questions concerning the person and work
of Christ answered, other questions do not seem quite so pressing and urgent.

A promise that still counts

That brings us to the fourth and final reason why we should
get to know Nathanael: he received a promise that still counts.

Nathanael would have been satisfied that day had he done
nothing more than meet the Messiah. But the Lord Jesus Christ
still had not finished with him. Nathanael had owned him as
the Messiah because Jesus had seen him sitting under the fig
tree. That was nothing compared to what Nathanael was about
to see. Jesus said, 'Most assuredly, I say to you, hereafter you
shall see heaven open, and the angels of God ascending and
descending upon the Son of Man' (John 1:51).

Jesus' terminology was not lost on Nathanael. It drew on
the story of the Old Testament patriarch, Jacob. While fleeing
from his brother Esau, Jacob had a vision in which he saw a
ladder extending to heaven and angels ascending and descending on it. The ladder Jacob saw was only a faint glimmer of the
coming Christ. He is the only true ladder between heaven and
earth. Leon Morris says Jesus is 'the link' between heaven and
earth and 'the means by which the realities of heaven are
brought down to earth'.[1]

Nathanael and the other disciples were destined to see Jesus
bringing heaven to earth. All through his ministry they would
see his heavenly power and grace.

The promise the Lord Jesus gave to Nathanael is one that all Christians may claim. We have, as he did, tasted of that heavenly power and grace, but, thank God, there is much more to come. The Lord Jesus even now says to all of his people, 'You will see greater things than these.' That promise will at last be fulfilled when he receives us unto himself in realms of eternal glory.

If we would receive these marvellously great and wonderful things, we must, as Nathanael did, break with our doubt and scepticism and embrace Christ with a true and living faith. We must join him in saying to Christ from our hearts, 'You are the Son of God! You are the King of Israel' (v. 49).

Ours is a day in which there is a distinct lack of definiteness about religious truth. We pride ourselves, not on our convictions, but rather on our doubts, and we frown upon those who claim to have certainty. Nothing so riles people today as for someone to claim that there is such a thing as absolute truth and that he or she has found it. We don't mind people searching for truth as long as they never arrive at it.

While the winds of tolerance and pluralism are steadily blowing, let the word go out that Nathanael's heartfelt confession must be ours if we hope to enter heaven at last. No one can be saved who is not definite in his conviction about the Lord Jesus Christ. The road that leads to eternal life has a narrow gate (Matt. 7:13-14). That gate is far too narrow for anyone to enter while armed with ambiguities and uncertainties.

17.
Saul of Tarsus: overcoming scepticism

Acts 9:1-9

If there was anything Saul of Tarsus was sure of, as he rode along the Damascus road under a blazing noonday sun, it was that Jesus of Nazareth was dead and buried somewhere.

It was that 'somewhere' that was causing all the problems. The garden tomb where Jesus' body was placed immediately after the crucifixion was empty. There was no doubt at all about that. The question was how it had come to be empty. The disciples of Jesus were joyfully alleging that he had risen from the dead, but Saul did not believe a word of it. As far as he and the other Pharisees were concerned, the tomb was empty because the disciples had managed to evade all the security, steal the body and hide it.

If he and his friends could just produce the body of Jesus, Saul was convinced that the spread of Christianity would come to a screeching halt. But as it was, the disciples of Jesus were so addled as to believe their own lie, and they were now filling Jerusalem and its environs with their crazy resurrection talk. Still worse, people were believing them. In the few short weeks after Pentecost thousands had come to believe that Jesus was indeed their long-awaited Messiah. Saul was greatly alarmed because this new sect was threatening everything he held near and dear. He and the other religious leaders had zealously promoted the teaching that one can only reach heaven by earning it through good works, and they had ordered their lives accordingly. But the disciples of Jesus insisted that salvation was not through good works at all, but it was rather a gift of God's grace, based on the dying and rising of this man Jesus. The idea that a man crucified in shame on a cross could be the Messiah and the means of salvation was to Saul too ludicrous for words.

It was clear to Saul, then, that something had to be done, and done at once. Since he and his fellow-Pharisees had not been able to find the body of Jesus, the next best thing, as far as Saul was concerned, was to persecute the disciples of Jesus to the point where they would have more to gain from refusing to preach than from preaching.

One of the leaders of the Christians, Stephen, had already been stoned to death (Acts 7:54-60), and Saul knew others were so fanatical that only execution could stop them. But, in his judgement, many could be persuaded to desist from their folly and cease the promulgation of their faith by spending some time in prison.

It was this grim business of executing and imprisoning that had fetched Saul out of Jerusalem and sent him on his way to Damascus (Acts 9:1-2). Saul was convinced that such stern measures would shortly be successful. After all, why would these people persist in a course that was going to prove so costly over nothing more than a dead body?

Visions of frightened Christians being led away in shackles were no doubt dancing in Saul's head as he drew near the city of Damascus. Suddenly, however, he was dazzled by a burst of light so brilliant that it made sunlight seem like darkness, a flash of light so resplendent that it blinded him and caused him to fall to the ground. While he was writhing in agony in the dust he heard a voice asking, 'Saul, Saul, why are you persecuting me?' (v. 4).

What was going on here? Was Saul having a violent reaction to some medication? Was he, as some have suggested, experiencing some sort of seizure? Had he allowed those he considered to be mad to drive him to madness as well? No, what happened to Saul on the Damascus Road was this: the Lord Jesus Christ intercepted him and brought him to the faith he had set out to destroy!

Saul of Tarsus learned three truths on the Damascus Road that day, truths all of those who are still apart from Christ urgently need to take home to their hearts.

The indisputable reality of Christ's resurrection

The evidence Saul encountered

First, Saul learned the resurrection of Jesus was not merely the fanciful imaginings of deluded men but was, in fact, an indisputable reality.

After he fell to the ground and heard the voice calling his name, Saul cried out, 'Who are you, Lord?' (v. 5). Imagine his surprise when he heard these words: 'I am Jesus, whom you are persecuting' (v. 5).

Although it is not mentioned in this passage, we know there was more to this experience than Saul simply hearing Jesus speak. He made it clear in later explanations of this experience that he actually saw the risen Jesus (1 Cor. 9:1; 15:8). This is a crucial point. The voice would, at the most, have proved that the spirit of Jesus was alive, but it would not necessarily have proved that his body had come out of the grave.

Can you imagine what went racing through his mind when he heard those words and saw that form? His first thought must have been that it could not possibly be Jesus of Nazareth, who was dead and buried. But hard on the heels of that thought would have come another: if Jesus was dead how could he be seeing and hearing him?

The conclusion Saul reached

It hit Saul at that instant that he had been totally wrong about Jesus. Alexander Maclaren graphically states it: 'The overwhelming conviction was flooded into his soul, that the Jesus whom he had thought of as a blasphemer, falsely alleged to have risen from the dead, lived in heavenly glory, amid celestial brightness too dazzling for human eyes.'[1]

Isn't it interesting that Saul saw the risen Lord while he was blind? Up to this point, Saul thought he saw clearly the truth about Jesus, but now, in his blindness, he realized he had not seen the truth at all. While he was seeing he was blind, but now that he was blind he saw.

Many are like Saul of Tarsus. They think they see clearly on the issue of Christianity. Mention it to them and they waste no time offering their opinions and making their pronouncements. They proudly ride along life's road in supreme confidence that Christianity is all a hoax that has been cleverly perpetrated upon the human race. Despite all the evidence to the contrary, they insist on believing the body of Jesus is still in that grave 'somewhere' where the disciples hid it long ago.

If you are a Saul of Tarsus, filled with yourself and your own opinions, I urge you to stop long enough to consider the possibility that you just might be wrong. Saul did not think he was wrong, but he was. And if you deny the resurrection of Christ, you are just as wrong as he was. It does not matter what most people think about Jesus. Even a multitude can be wrong. Only one thing matters, and that is the evidence. Have you ever thoroughly weighed it? Before you pronounce on Christianity, please weigh it carefully. How do you explain the empty tomb? How do you explain the experiences of the hundreds who saw the resurrected Jesus? How do you explain the disciples of Jesus being transformed from frightened cowards into fiery evangelists? An honest and candid appraisal of such evidence yields only one conclusion — that the Lord Jesus Christ arose.

Scepticism hurts those who hold it

The second truth Saul learned on the road to Damascus may be put in this way: those who deny the resurrection do so to their own hurt.

The living Christ said to the smitten Saul, 'It is hard for you to kick against the goads' (Acts 9:5). The Lord's reference here was to ox-goads, sharp spikes that were fastened to the front of ox-carts. If an ox decided to register his unhappiness about having to pull the cart by kicking at it, those ox-goads would quickly convince him that it was more painful to kick than to pull. It was a stupid ox that would keep kicking when each kick brought a painful jab from those spikes.

Up to this point Saul had been behaving very much like a stupid ox. He had been kicking with all his might against the cart of Christianity, thinking that with each kick he was damaging it, but he was in reality only hurting himself.

How did Saul's denial of Christ's resurrection hurt him? The answer is that it put him at war with the very God he professed to serve. Time after time the Bible tells us that it was God himself who raised Jesus from the dead (1 Cor. 6:14; 15:15; Gal. 1:1; 1 Thess. 1:10; 1 Peter 1:21). The resurrection was nothing less than God putting his stamp of approval upon the life and death of Jesus and declaring him to be God in human flesh (Rom. 1:4). Saul was himself to write later that Jesus was raised from the dead that 'in all things he may have the pre-eminence' (Col. 1:18).

The point is that if God has invested so much in the life and death of Jesus, it is utter folly for a mere mortal to reject Jesus.

Going to war against God simply cuts us off from all hope for the life to come, and it stores up his wrath until it finally breaks loose with all its fury on the Day of Judgement. God is the one with whom we all have to deal, and he will not be kindly disposed to those who have rejected the one he has designated Lord of all. If God has designated Jesus as the bridge from this life to eternal life, a person is a fool if he ignores that bridge.

Jesus is worthy of service

The final truth Saul learned on the Damascus road was the need to serve this one who had encountered him. No sooner had the Lord finished speaking than Saul asked, 'Lord, what do you want me to do?' (Acts 9:6). His question reveals that he had in the space of just a few seconds come to this logical argument: 'If Jesus is risen from the dead, he is Lord. If he is Lord, I am his servant. If I am his servant, I must find out what he expects me to do.' Such simple and profound logic! It is so simple that it would seem that millions would be asking Saul's question: 'Lord, what do you want me to do?' But, amazingly enough, there are millions who claim to believe in the resurrection of Jesus and yet have not followed the implications of it through to the point of living in obedience to the living Lord.

This, I confess, is a source of amazement to me. I am amazed at those who, in the face of all the evidence, stubbornly refuse to believe in the resurrection of Jesus. But I am even more amazed at those who say they believe it and yet do not have any desire to live for Christ. I can only say that such people have only an intellectual belief in the resurrection and have not truly encountered the living Saviour.

Section IV
Pictures of perils in the Christian life

Coming to faith in Christ does not bring us to the end of pitfalls and dangers. It rather means facing another set of perils, ones that are unique to the Christian life.

Satan's first design is always to keep sinners from the knowledge of Christ. If he fails there, he shifts to another strategy — that of hindering Christians in their service to the Lord.

We only have to look at the church of Corinth to see how remarkably successful Satan can be in his effort to entrap and enfeeble Christians. This was a church in the grip of multiple temptations and dangers. The Christian life called for discipline, drive and determination, but they believed in comfort, ease and self-gratification.

It fell to the apostle Paul to correct those erring believers and to challenge them to run faithfully and diligently the race the Lord had set before them, the race of the Christian life (1 Cor. 9:24). He sets before them his own example (1 Cor. 9:26-27), which was positive in nature. The Corinthians were to do as he was doing. Then he moves to reinforce his teaching by citing a negative example, the example of Israel under Moses. The Israelites failed to be disciplined and diligent in the race God had set before them and, in so doing, had brought terrible calamities upon themselves. Paul very pointedly states his purpose in calling Israel to the attention of the Corinthians:

'Now all these things happened to them as examples, and they were written for our admonition...' (1 Cor. 10:11).

What Paul said of Israel may very well be said of all those we meet in the Old Testament. They are examples to us. Sometimes the example is negative; it shows us how not to live. Sometimes the example is positive; it shows us how to live. As a matter of fact, we are in an even more advantageous position than the Corinthians. They had the same Old Testament examples as we have, but we have the examples of New Testament characters as well.

My purpose in these chapters is to take a tour through some of these examples and to gather lessons from them. By taking heed to these pictures from days gone by of perils we ourselves are facing, we can either avoid those pitfalls and dangers altogether, or discover how to escape from them.

18.
The people of Israel: a warning against idolatry

Exodus 32

The Old Testament is primarily concerned to document God's gracious dealings with his people. It may also be considered in a secondary fashion to document the unrelenting struggle of God's people against idolatry.

Joshua, Moses' successor as the leader of Israel, knew all about this struggle. In his farewell address to the nation, he challenged the people to stay true to the Lord: 'Now therefore, fear the Lord, serve him in sincerity and in truth, and put away the gods which your fathers served on the other side of the River and in Egypt. Serve the Lord!' (Josh. 24:14).

The river to which Joshua made reference was the Euphrates. Abraham, the father of the nation, lived in the land of Ur beyond the Euphrates when God called him into a covenant relationship with himself. Before God called him, he was an idolater (see Josh. 24:2).

Furthermore, as Joshua observed, the people of Israel had served false gods while they were in the land of Egypt. Because Joshua knew that idolatry would continue to be the bane of the nation, he sternly warned the people about the importance of remaining true to the Lord. Joshua's concern was well founded. The nation would eventually split into two kingdoms, and each of those kingdoms would be conquered by a foreign nation and carried away captive, and the primary reason for their destruction was idolatry (2 Kings 17:5-12; 22:16-17).

It is very likely that a certain episode was uppermost in Joshua's mind as he delivered his farewell address. He was on the mountain with Moses when the people suddenly bolted from the worship of God and built a golden calf (Exod. 24:13; 32:1-6).

The prelude to idolatry

If we are to comprehend the enormity of this plunge into idolatry, we must first get our bearings. The nation of Israel, under the leadership of Moses, had at this time been released from their bondage in Egypt only a very brief time (Exod. 19:1). They were encamped at the foot of Mt Sinai while Moses was meeting with the Lord on the mountain (Exod. 24:12).

The affirmation of the people

It is important for us to understand that Moses had already made one trip up the mountain, during which he received the Ten Commandments and other instructions. He had reported these to the people (Exod. 19:3,20-25; 24:3), who very readily embraced them with this resounding affirmation: 'All the words which the Lord has said we will do' (Exod. 24:3).

There was no ambiguity at all about the second of these commandments: 'You shall not make for yourself a carved image — any likeness of anything that is in heaven above, or that is in the earth beneath, or that is in the water under the earth; you shall not bow down to them nor serve them' (Exod. 20:4-5).

The incentives to obey

There was also no ambiguity about the terrible cost attached to disobeying this commandment. After stating it, the Lord had proceeded to add these words: 'For I, the Lord your God, am a jealous God, visiting the iniquity of the fathers upon the children to the third and fourth generations of those who hate me, but showing mercy to thousands, to those who love me and keep my commandments' (Exod. 20:5).

If those words did not provide enough incentive for the people of Israel to obey this commandment, all they had to do was review the recent expressions of God's goodness to them. He had delivered them from grinding, oppressive bondage in Egypt and had borne them to himself on 'eagles' wings' (Exod. 19:4). Furthermore, he had promised to make them his own special treasure, a kingdom of priests and a holy nation (Exod. 19:5-6).

Such kindness in the past coupled with such a promise for the future would appear to make obedience to God's commandments the delight of every Israelite heart, but the clarity of the commandment, the incentives to obey it and their own hearty endorsement of it were not sufficient for these hearts. Only forty days (Exod. 24:18) after Moses again ascended the mountain, the people gathered around Aaron and began clamouring for him to lead the way in a flagrant rebellion against the second commandment.

The cause of their idolatry

What possessed them to do such a thing? They pleaded the absence of Moses (v. 1). To them it was unthinkable that he could be gone so long and still return. This was a quite remarkable assumption in the light of how God had used Moses. Moses had announced their deliverance from Egypt (Exod. 6:5-7) and assured them that they would receive the land promised to their fathers (Exod. 6:8). He was also the instrument God used to rain plagues down upon Pharaoh and all of Egypt (Exod. 7:14 - 12:30). And Moses actually led the people out of Egypt and into the Sinaitic wilderness (Exod. 12:31-39; 13:17 - 14:31).

All of this would seem to indicate that God was not about to set Moses aside before the task of bringing the people to the land promised to them was complete. But the people of Israel were not interested in thinking deeply and seriously about God's dealings with them or about what those dealings suggested — that is, that their God was entirely faithful.

The truth is that the absence of Moses did not really matter that much to them. It just happened to be a handy pretext for them to put into practice what was in their hearts. And what was that? If we jump forward several centuries to the book of Acts, we find the godly Stephen giving an inspired account of the golden-calf episode, and he has nothing at all to say about the absence of Moses. He does, however, offer this telling explanation: 'In their hearts they turned back to Egypt' (Acts 7:39). The absence of Moses was, then, nothing more than a convenient outward reality which served as an excuse for them to yield to the promptings of an inner reality — hearts that were still in Egypt.

Egypt was all these people knew and, as Joshua was to state plainly, many of them had served the visible gods of Egypt (Josh. 24:14). Now they were away from Egypt and called upon to serve an invisible God, a God of such consuming holiness that they could not approach him without Moses as their mediator. Perhaps it was the desire to have what Michael Horton calls 'a greasy familiarity' with God[1] that caused them to yearn for gods such as they had worshipped in Egypt. As far as they were concerned, Moses' absence gave them the perfect opportunity to satisfy that yearning. So they put the proposition to Aaron (Exod. 32:1), the golden calf was made (vv. 2-4) and a celebration was held (vv. 5-6), which had more to do with sex than religion (the Hebrew word translated 'rose up to play' is also used in Genesis 26:8 where it definitely has sexual overtones).

A vigorous debate centres around the question of whether the people thought of this golden calf as a new god, or only as a new and better way to worship the God who had brought them out of Egypt. Stephen's statement in the book of Acts indicates that they were thinking in terms of the gods they had worshipped in Egypt and were, therefore, embracing a new god. But it is noteworthy that Aaron proclaimed the day of celebration by using the covenant name for God (Exod. 32:5). It is possible, therefore, that some of the people thought of the calf in one way while others thought of it in another way.

Even if most of the people viewed this calf as a new and improved way of worshipping the true God, they were dreadfully mistaken. The calf, or bull, a symbol of power, was obviously intended to honour the power of God. But any image of God does the exact opposite of what it is intended to do. It obscures rather than reveals God. The golden calf could not do justice to God's power which, unlike the calf's, is unlimited. And the image of the calf completely excluded all the other attributes of God. God is more than power. He is also omnipresent, omniscient, holy, just, wise, merciful, gracious, faithful and eternal. The calf was, therefore, actually derogatory to the very one it purported to honour because it reduced him to one minimal aspect of his personality and confined him to a single location.

Nothing is more distressing and pathetic in all of this than Aaron's role. Given the opportunity to stand for God and truth in this situation, he meekly complied with the desire of the people (Exod. 32:2-5) and, when called to account by Moses, lamely explained that he just threw the gold in the fire and the calf miraculously emerged (vv. 21-24).

The cost of their idolatry

It all came screeching to a halt with a crushing judgement of immense proportions (vv. 25-28). After burning the calf and reducing it to powder, Moses sprinkled it in water and forced the people to drink it (v. 20). All of this was designed to drive the utter helplessness of their god home to the Israelites. A god that cannot keep itself from being burnt and ground to powder is not much of a god. A god that can be drunk by its devotees is even less than they are. Imagine having a god that can be worshipped one moment and drunk the next!

Current expressions of idolatry

Naked Israelites dancing feverishly around a golden calf — it all sounds very crude and far removed from us, but it is not. Calves are still emerging from the fire. When we give to any object or person the allegiance and devotion that belong to God alone, we are guilty of idolatry. If we put money before God, we have an idol. If we put pleasure before God, we have an idol. It is the same with our careers and our families.

Idolatry can be even more subtle. When we make the God of the Bible to conform to our own liking, we have an idol.

There is not a hair-breadth's of change in the true God since that day all those centuries ago. He is still the God of burning glory and holiness and, just as Israel of old could not approach him except through the mediatorial work of Moses, so we can know him only through the true mediator whom Moses was intended to foreshadow. That mediator is none other than the Lord Jesus Christ (1 Tim. 2:5).

But this is not the kind of God people want these days. We want the God who is user-friendly and seeker-sensitive. As the Israelites thought of themselves as being sovereign in the area of worship, so it is easy for us to think of ourselves in the same way. We pride ourselves on knowing what is best and what 'sells'. And a majestic, glorious God who is clothed in mystery and condemns sin is not what sells. A God who insists that there is only one way of salvation, and that way is the redeeming work of his Son on a bloody Roman cross, is not what people want to hear about. What sells is a God who is tame and non-threatening, one who is not concerned about our serving him, but with serving us. What people want is a God who busies himself with helping us manage the problems and circumstances of our lives. We are not concerned that God should bring us safely into eternity, but only that he should get us comfortably through another week. And preachers and churches, who, following the sad example set by Aaron, are ever anxious to please, are dumbing down the message and taking away God's glory in order to give people what they want. Worship services are light and cheery. Reverence is considered to be outdated and laughable. Holiness, faithfulness, commitment, responsibility and discipline are regarded as obscene words. References to sin, guilt, condemnation and a blood atonement are muted.

Even though there is much in the modern-day church to lament, there is still consolation and hope. There is a mediator, the Lord Jesus Christ. He is still at the right hand of God to make intercession for his people, and when they come to their senses, see their idolatry and repent of it, they can, because of his work, find forgiveness and renewal (1 John 2:1).

19.
Achan: the danger of selfish individualism

Joshua 6:18-19; 7:1,19-22

Now we come to a man whose name will be tarnished and besmirched as long as time endures. His name was Achan. He was a man who had been abundantly blessed by God. He had seen God do marvellous things in his nation of Israel. He had seen God's Word indisputably confirmed on more than one occasion. He had seen the generation that God miraculously delivered from Egypt fall one by one in the wilderness because of their refusal to believe God (Num. 14:26-38). He had seen the Jordan river roll up and the new generation of Israelites cross over into the land of Canaan on dry ground just as God had promised (Josh. 3:1-17). And he had, along with his countrymen, stood in stunned wonder as the walls of the mighty fortress of Jericho crashed to the ground in front of them just as God had promised (Josh. 6:1-27).

God is not to be trifled with

Yes, Achan had seen it all, and if there was any one lesson to be learned from all he had seen, it was that this God who was at work in Israel must not be trifled with. This was the eternal God with mighty power who had demonstrated again and again a jealous regard for his Word. If he said something would happen, it did. And this is the God who had stoutly proclaimed that the obedience of his people would be rewarded with indescribable blessings and their disobedience would be met with unspeakable anguish and woe (Deut. 28:15-68).

Before the people of Israel ever went up against Jericho, God made his will about what was to happen to the spoils of the city as plain as the noonday sun. They were all consecrated to the Lord and were to be put in his treasury (Josh. 6:18-19).

God was, of course, entitled to make this demand. It was he who had brought their fathers out from under the tyranny of Pharaoh. He was the one who had faithfully sustained them in the wilderness during all the years of their wandering. He was the one who had parted the waters of the Jordan. And he was the one who was now giving the impregnable city of Jericho into the hands of his people.

There were plenty of other cities to be conquered and plenty of spoils for the people to claim as their own (Josh. 8:2), but Jericho belonged in a special and peculiar way to the Lord. It stood as the gateway to the whole land, and the Lord wanted its conquest to inscribe a distinct and indelible message on the consciousness of his people. The method of the conquest was designed to show them the truth of his grace. They did nothing to cause Jericho to fall but simply received it as a gift from God. By bringing all the spoils to God the people would show that they understood that such a gracious God is worthy of wholehearted obedience.

God had also made something else plain before the people made their final, dramatic marches around Jericho: if anyone violated God's command about the spoils he would bring calamity, not just upon himself, but upon the whole nation (Josh. 6:18). The whole nation was to be held responsible for the disobedience of any individuals.

Why would God hold all accountable for the actions of a few? I think we have to say God had a great cause he wanted to achieve through the whole nation, a cause that could not succeed if individuals did not put that cause and the welfare of the whole nation above their own interests. By holding the nation accountable for individual actions God showed that each Israelite was part of something much bigger than himself.

Achan and all his countrymen had all this in place, then, before the walls of Jericho ever toppled to the ground. And the faithfulness of God to his Word had been so forcefully driven home on so many occasions that one would have thought that, before rushing over the crumbled walls into the city, each man would have said to himself, 'I must not take any of the spoils for myself. God is not to be trifled with.'

Achan's flagrant disregard for God's law

Achan may very well have said the same to himself, but he found it impossible to adhere to that resolve. There in the spoils was a beautiful Babylonian garment, the likes of which he had never seen before. And right there beside it were two hundred shekels of silver and a wedge of pure gold. Immediately Achan scooped them up. These would have to go to their commander Joshua as part of the Lord's treasury. But suddenly he stopped. No one was with him when he found these items, and no one had seen him gather them up. It would be really easy just to hide them in his tent instead of taking them to Joshua. He was sure he could do it and no one would be any the wiser. He quickly made his way to his tent. Just one gentle reminder of God's word from his wife or from a son or daughter would have brought him to his senses, but they were all delighted by what he had done and helped him stow away the loot. Their future in the new land now seemed to be secure.

The essence of Achan's act

Why did Achan do it? What drove him to such reckless behaviour? Think of it in these terms. Here was the choice that confronted him: he could take the goods to Joshua, which would bring honour and glory to God and promote the well-being of God's people, or he could keep the goods for himself, which would bring him personal happiness and fulfilment.

By keeping the goods for himself, then, Achan was putting his personal happiness above the glory of God and the welfare of God's people. He did it because gratifying his personal desires was more important to him than the law of God and the welfare of the people of God.

He would not, of course, have stated it in such stark terms. Had we been able, while he was making his choice, to invisibly hover over him and put an ear against the wall of his inmost thoughts, we probably would have heard him saying, 'What possible harm could there be in taking just a few goods for myself? There will still be plenty left for the Lord.' Or perhaps we would have heard him saying to himself, 'Achan, old friend, you have already done a lot for the Lord. You deserve a break today.'

If those were indeed Achan's thoughts, he was guilty of holding one of the trademark beliefs of our age, which is that personal happiness and fulfilment should override every other consideration. In his book *What Americans Believe*, George Barna documents this. He says that two-thirds of all American adults say the purpose of life is enjoyment and personal fulfilment. From this Barna concludes: 'Americans typically view life as a temporary effort to obtain all the satisfaction and pleasure possible during their tenure on this planet.'[1]

This mentality has devastating ramifications for society in general, but it is particularly damaging when it crops up in the church. After all, the people of God are in a situation not unlike the one Israel of old was in. Just as God clearly made his will known to them regarding the spoils of Jericho, so he has made his will known to us on a wide array of matters. And just as he prized those people and desired to work through them, so he prizes the church today. He has purchased her at a very dear price, the blood of his Son, Jesus Christ. He tenderly regards her as a father does his children. She is the apple of his eye and her name is inscribed on the palms of his hands.

God has not changed in his nature or in his fundamental purposes since that long-ago day in devastated Jericho. He still wants us to bring glory to his name by obeying his commands. And he still wants us to join him in prizing the welfare of his people and to do those things that will promote it. He wants us to see that his purpose or cause for the church is larger than ourselves, and he wants us to love her and live for her. John Calvin expressed the place the church ought to have in our estimation in these words: 'He cannot have God for his Father who does not take the church for his mother.'

Once we understand these fundamental realities we can see that the story of Achan is not just a boring bit of ancient history. His choice is still being played out in our own age. Any time we let our own desires and happiness crowd out obedience to God we have donned Achan's Babylonian garment and pocketed his Canaanite shekels.

How many professing Christians have made Achan's choice on this matter of worshipping God Sunday by Sunday? How many, knowing full well that their presence in the house of God would both bring honour to his name and promote the well-being of his people, deliberately choose to stay away to do something they want to do? How many professing Christians say on the Lord's Day, 'This is the only day I have for myself,' or, 'This is my day to be with my family'?

'But doesn't God want us to be happy?' The person who asks this question always expects 'Yes' for an answer and prepares to then say, 'Well, I know what makes me happy,' and to enumerate two or three things that are contrary to God's commands. Perhaps Achan employed this reasoning as he gazed upon the forbidden goods: 'I know what God said, but, surely, he wants me to be happy, and these items would really make me happy.'

The great flaw in that reasoning is that we know what makes us happy and we assume that God must, therefore, simply acquiesce and let us do our thing. Yes, we do know what gives us momentary pleasure, but God, on the other hand, is interested in our eternal happiness, not just what gives us pleasure for the moment.

Because Achan and his family refused to live for the honour of God and the good of God's people they paid a terrible price (Josh. 7:24-26). No, God does not use such severe judgements in the temporal realm on everyone who puts personal happiness above God's cause. As a matter of fact, many who live exclusively for their personal happiness seem to fare quite well. But such severe temporal judgements are designed to show the far greater eternal judgement that awaits all those who put themselves above God. This is, in fact, how Jesus applied some of the catastrophes that befell people during his ministry (Luke 13:1-5).

We must, therefore, beware of following in Achan's footsteps. Our true happiness lies in obeying God and in seeking the welfare of his people, not in living as if our own individual enjoyment in the here and now is all that matters.

20.
Samson: the lure of a seductive culture

Judges 16:4-5,15-21

Our word 'seduction' comes from the Latin word *'seducere'* which literally means 'to lead away'. The word has a negative connotation — that is, it implies that one is led away from something that is good and upright to something that is base and vile. In other words, it not only means to be led away, but to be led astray.

We cannot think long about someone being seduced without Samson coming to mind. He is the great victim of seduction of all times. To appreciate what a tragic figure he is, and what a terrible thing his seduction was, we have to begin with the calling from which he strayed.

Samson's calling

The fact is that Samson was called to be a special instrument of God at a time when the people of God as a whole had been seduced by Philistine culture. During the period of the judges, the nation of Israel found herself oppressed by her wicked, cruel neighbours on several occasions. But in each of those instances we are told that the people of Israel 'cried unto the Lord' (Judg. 3:9,15; 4:3; 6:6-7; 10:10). However, when we

come to the period of time in which the Philistines had su-
premacy over Israel we read nothing of the people crying out
to God. R. C. Sproul says, 'Unlike previous invaders, the
Philistines were cultured and not terribly oppressive; thus, Israel relaxed under their domination and did not cry out to the
Lord.'[1]

This, then, was the situation into which God called Samson.
The people of Israel had settled down into a peaceful co-existence with the Philistines, and Samson was to be God's instrument for stirring up his people and calling them away from
their infatuation with Philistine culture. To this end, God commanded Samson's parents that he was to be a Nazirite. He
was not to have his hair shaved and he was not to drink any
wine or eat anything unclean (Judg. 13:5,7).

Endowed with superhuman strength, Samson was for a long
time a powerful and effective instrument in the hands of God.
As we read the account of his life, we find the refrain: 'The
Spirit of the Lord came mightily upon him' (Judg. 14:6,19;
15:14). This tells us where the real strength of Samson lay.
His hair was the outer symbol of his consecration to God and
his strength, but the source of that strength was the Spirit of
God. James B. Jordan writes, 'There was no magical tie between Samson's strength and his hair, but there was a spiritual
connection in that God gives strength to those who are dedicated to him, and in Samson's case, his dedicated head was
the sign of his separation to God.'[2]

After years of being used of God in a mighty and wonderful way, we might expect Samson to be unconquerable. He
had seen God achieve great victories through him time after
time, and he would seem to be as strong in faith as he was in
physical strength. The very last thing we would expect to learn
is that Samson would flirt with losing the strength that God
had given and used.

Samson's collapse

Enter Delilah. Most think she was a Philistine herself. Others think she was an apostate Israelite. The Bible does not say. One thing is clear: she was a Philistine in her heart, and she so identified with the Philistines that she must be counted as one.

Delilah must have been stunningly beautiful, and the Philistine lords, knowing Samson had a weakness for beautiful women, enlisted her in their cause. She would, for a substantial sum, find out the source of Samson's strength, and the Philistine lords would lurk in another room. At the proper moment they would step in and overpower him. When will children of God ever learn that there are always enemies lurking nearby waiting for a moment of weakness so they can move in and destroy?

Three times Delilah asked Samson to reveal the source of his strength. Three times Samson gave her a false answer. Three times the Philistines rushed in to take him, only to be overpowered themselves, but there is no mention in any of these encounters about the Spirit of God coming mightily upon Samson. Because of Samson's mad flirtation with sin, the Lord had already departed from him (Judg. 16:20).

Finally, Delilah pestered Samson beyond his ability to endure, and he revealed the true source of his strength. When he fell asleep, she cut the long locks of his hair, the Philistines moved in, overpowered him and led him away (vv. 19-21).

Does this story seem to be too far-fetched to be believed? Why, after it was obvious what Delilah had in mind, did Samson continue even to see her, let alone talk to her about the source of his strength? Why would he take such a terrible risk? Here we see the dreadful weakness of human nature. This was not just true of Samson; it is true of all of us. We flirt with things that we know will destroy us. Tell me how many times you have been burned by sin and gone right back to it, and I will tell you why Samson kept going back to Delilah.

Samson paid a dreadful price for his folly. The Philistines gouged his eyes out and put him to grinding in a mill. This was their way of showing that their god, Dagon, the god of grain, had won the victory over the God of Israel. Likewise, when a child of God falls, the unbelieving world is always quick to gloat over him and attribute his failure to an inherent flaw in Christianity.

Samson's final victory

Their victory was short-lived. While Samson was grinding in the mill, his hair grew and his repentance with it. When the Philistines brought him to one of their drunken festivals, Samson's strength had returned to the point where he was able to pull the pillars of the building down to kill himself and the Philistines (Judg. 16:25-30).

How did Samson get into such a mess? How did he lose his strength? By taking things for granted? By not walking in obedience to God? By seeing how close he could get to the fire without being burned? All of these things and more came into play, but the final answer is that he himself became so enamoured with the Philistine culture as embodied in, and expressed by, Delilah that he was blind to everything else.

I don't know what epitaph his relatives put on his tombstone after they dragged his body out of the rubble of the Philistine temple, but I know what they could have written: seduced by a culture that was opposed to his God.

Samson's message for the church

A message of caution

Samson is a very fitting and appropriate picture of the church today. We, like him, have been called to influence our culture for Christ. We are called to be salt to slow the moral decay of the kingdom of man and light to show the way to God's kingdom.

But the culture we are trying to influence is not a passive culture. It has its own doctrine, its own agenda and its own preachers, and it is militantly and aggressively dedicated to resisting our message and spreading its own.

Most of us do quite well for a while in being faithful to God and in standing against the agenda of the world. But the continual, seductive wooing of Delilah begins to wear down our defences, and before we know what has happened we are thinking and talking like the Philistines of this world. No, the unbelievers of this world are not wrong in everything they believe, say and do, but when they say, 'Live for yourself' or 'Live for the moment,' or 'There is no such thing as absolute truth,' they are advocating doctrines that brazenly contradict the teachings of the Word of God.

The power of Christianity is in that Word, and when we allow ourselves to be seductively carried away from it, we, like Samson, will find ourselves robbed of power and humiliated before a taunting world. Samson stands as a lasting reminder that even the strongest will fall if he goes whoring after pagan culture, and such whoring always leads to powerlessness, blindness and death. Is this not the explanation for the feebleness that keeps the church from seeing mighty movings of the Spirit of God? Is this not the explanation for the blindness that keeps the church from being able to discern what is true and what is false? Is this not the explanation for the deadness that keeps the church from rejoicing in the reality of spiritual things?

A message of consolation

The picture of Samson is as pathetic as any could be, but there is also great hope and consolation to be found in his story. In the final analysis, the Philistines did not overpower Samson because they were stronger but because he was faithless. Christians sometimes fall into the trap of thinking the godless culture that surrounds them is their greatest enemy. Godless culture is, of course, an enemy, but only in a secondary sense. Our greatest enemy is ourselves. If we are oppressed today, it is not because this world's beliefs and lifestyle are stronger than we are, but because we have been faithless to the God who makes us strong.

How we need to take this home to our hearts! Our calling is to be faithful to God! But what about the child of God who has already been unfaithful? What about the Christian who has been seduced by mistaken beliefs? Thank God, there is another consolation from the life of Samson for such a case! Spiritual hair always grows back! The child of God may be seduced by his pagan culture, but he will ultimately come back to the Lord, and be renewed. And, as Samson was finally vindicated, so each child of God is going to be ultimately vindicated. There is coming a blessed day when we shall be taken out of the culture that despises the things of God, we shall shine as the stars of the sky for ever, and the whole universe will know that we were right to walk with God.

21.
David: living under the burden of guilt

Psalm 32:1-6

No burden is heavier than the burden of guilt, and perhaps no one has ever carried a heavier burden of guilt than King David.

We know his story all too well. He — the man after God's own heart, the man who had been enormously blessed, the man who had the keen spiritual insights we find in the psalms — committed unspeakably vile and callous acts. He lusted after his neighbour's wife, committed adultery with her and had her husband killed to cover it all up (2 Sam. 11).

After Uriah was dead and Bathsheba was 'lawfully' his wife, David must have heaved a great sigh of relief. He thought he had successfully hidden his treacherous acts. What he had really done was release into his life the hounds of guilt, hounds that pursued him every waking moment and, we may be sure, even in his sleep. Hounds of hell they were!

In Psalm 32, David describes how he felt when he was relentlessly dogged by guilt:

When I kept silent, my bones grew old
Through my groaning all the day long.
For day and night your hand was heavy upon me;
My vitality was turned into the drought of summer

(vv. 3-4).

Ageing, constant groaning, heaviness, drought are graphic terms. David found it necessary to use these terms because of the guilt he felt.

Every child of God knows about this. We have not all done exactly what David did, but we have all grappled with the monster of guilt. The well-known author Noel Coward is said to have decided as a prank to send the following note to twenty of the most famous men in London: 'Everybody has found out what you are doing. If I were you I would get out of town.' All twenty left town![1]

We all feel guilty about something. Perhaps we cheated someone in order to get ahead. Perhaps we failed to help someone who desperately needed help. Maybe we violated our marriage vows and engaged in a clandestine affair. Perhaps we did not give the proper time to our children, and when we did give them some time, we were grumpy and irritable. Perhaps we have taken God's day as our own to do with as we please. Perhaps we regularly take God's name in vain. Perhaps we have nurtured unclean thoughts by viewing a pornographic film or magazine. Or perhaps it is a combination of several things.

Yes, we all know about guilt. What we do not always know is how to find relief from it. David can help us with this. On the basis of his experience, we can first say there is relief in understanding why we feel guilty.

The meaning of guilt

What is guilt? The dictionary defines it as 'the state of one who has violated a law'. It defines the word 'guilty' in this way: 'one judged as an offender against the law'.

In order for there to be guilt, then, there must be an objective standard of right and wrong. The Bible insists that God's law is that standard.

David alludes to God's standard of behaviour by the words he uses for his sin. He calls it 'transgression' (Ps. 32:1), which indicates the stepping over a known boundary. He calls it 'sin' (v. 1), which refers to missing a mark or a target. He calls it 'iniquity' (v. 2), which carries the idea of twisting something.

In each case, the thought is the same — namely, failing to live up to a standard. There is a boundary, a target, something that is straight and true, but sin steps over the boundary, misses the target and twists what is straight.

This brings us to the glaring contradiction running right through the middle of our society. On one hand, we have heroically tried to eliminate the idea of an objective standard of right and wrong, opting for a relativism that says it all depends on the individual and his situation. On the other hand, guilt is running amok.

How are we to explain this contradiction? It should be obvious that eliminating the standard of right and wrong is not an easy matter. It is written inside us. We all innately, intuitively know that there is a God, that he has given us certain laws by which to live and that we have fallen far short of those laws.

But how does this understanding of guilt help us? In this way: it tells us we can avoid guilt by doing what God wants us to do. Here is where the rub comes in: we want it both ways. We want to break God's laws and not feel guilty about it, but it does not work that way.

The cure for guilt

A second lesson we can learn from David is not to deny our guilt but openly confess it to God. David found relief when he did this. He says to the Lord:

I acknowledged my sin to you,
And my iniquity I have not hidden.
I said, 'I will confess my transgressions to the Lord,'
And you forgave the iniquity of my sin

(Ps. 32:5).

What does it mean to confess our sins? It means to agree with God about them. Before David came to the point of confession, he and God were on opposite sides of the fence. God was condemning his sin, and he was defending himself by rationalizing and excusing his sin. When he finally came to the point of confession, David stopped fighting against God. He, as it were, walked over to God's side of the fence and stood with God and joined him in condemning his own sin.

The acceptance of God's forgiveness

Another lesson we can learn from David's experience is to accept God's forgiveness. He says to the Lord, 'You forgave the iniquity of my sin' (v. 5). That is the language of triumphant certainty. It does not admit any doubt or reservation. David does not say he hopes he is forgiven, but he flatly affirms that he has been forgiven.

How did David know God had forgiven him? The answer is quite simple. He knew God had promised always to forgive his children when they sincerely repent of their sins. He says to the Lord in another place, 'For you, Lord, are good, and ready to forgive, and abundant in mercy to all those who call upon you' (Ps. 86:5).

But the promise of God to forgive his repenting people must be believed. This is the point at which many of God's people go astray. Even though they have God's promise to forgive them, they cannot forgive themselves. So they keep dredging up their sin and feeling guilty about it. And Satan gets the victory because, while they are feeling guilty over their sin, they are virtually useless to the cause of Christ.

What shall we say to such people? God has told us that when we repent of our sins, he casts them as far as the east is from the west (Ps. 103:12), never to be remembered again (Jer. 31:34).

Our word, then, to our troubled brother or sister who will not let go of his or her guilt is this: 'Dear brother, dear sister, believe God. Don't try to resurrect what he has buried. If God says you are forgiven, you are forgiven. Rejoice in it.' Refusal to do so indicates the presence of a very common tendency — to function on the basis of our feelings rather than on the basis of the Word of God.

Feelings in religion are wonderful and should not be denigrated. Most of us could profit from deeper feelings about the things of God! But feelings must always be brought under the authority of the Word of God. They are not to be the engine that pulls the train of spirituality. The Word of God is the engine. Feelings are the carriages that follow behind.

When we get down to the nub of the matter, it is highly insulting to God for us to refuse to believe what he has said. It is rather sheer pride and arrogance to cling to our guilt when God has promised to forgive those who repent.

If God has pledged to forgive, we must forgive ourselves. It has often been said that those who refuse to learn from history are doomed to repeat it. We have in David a very clear history on this matter of guilt. If we ignore it, we doom ourselves to walk the same miserable path he walked. The course of wisdom is to learn from him, to learn what creates guilt and to avoid it, to learn to confess our sin and to accept God's gracious forgiveness.

22.
The psalmists: dealing with the troubled heart

Psalms 55:6; 57:1; 102:6

The first two of the psalms cited above are credited to David. No author is named for the third, although many Bible students find it to be very much like the psalms of David. While these psalms may very well have had different authors, they also have striking similarities. They were each written in a time of serious trouble.

The pelican

The author of Psalm 102 chose a particularly picturesque way of stating his problem. He says, 'I am like a pelican of the wilderness.' He also likens himself to an owl in the desert and a sparrow on the housetop. He was so troubled, so burdened, that he felt completely out of his element, in the same way as the pelican is out of its element when it is away from water. Beyond that, the psalmist felt utterly alone and desolate and even found himself moaning with a sound similar to that of the pelican or the owl. This is a very despondent and burdened man.

We know something about burdens ourselves. To be burdened is to be conscious of carrying a heavy load. It calls to mind the image of a beast being laden down with goods, or a ship being filled with merchandise. If we feel something pressing us or taxing our resources, we can say we have a burden.

Some burdens are light and momentary. Others are exceedingly heavy and seemingly unending, so much so that we find ourselves easily identifying with the psalmist and his pelican imagery. If we were to be completely candid about it, many of us would have to admit that we have the pelican problem. We feel utterly alone and helpless, and our hearts are so heavy that we find ourselves softly moaning as we journey along. Our burdens are such that the wilderness seems to be a very fitting image indeed for this world in which we live. I have served as a pastor for many years now, and the people of God (and their pastors) seem to me to be more burdened than at any time in my ministry.

We know we should not be burdened and distressed, or at least we know we should not be burdened and distressed by many of the things that do weigh us down (there are indeed legitimate burdens for the Christian to bear). We know the Scriptures tell us to be joyful, and we know that we have an abundance of reasons for rejoicing. We know we have more benefits and more ease than any generation in the history of humanity. We know that constant heaviness exacts a heavy toll. It keeps us from being at our best for our Lord, our church and our families. We know that those who do not know the Lord are constantly watching Christians and forming conclusions about Christianity by what they see, or do not see, in us. We know our time on this earth is short and that we ought to be giving ourselves to the service of the Lord without being weighed down by discouragement. But, knowing all of these things, the people of God often find themselves discouraged, distressed and despondent. Why is this the case? Why are so many Christians burdened and troubled? And what can be done about it?

David was feeling the 'pelican problem' when he wrote Psalm 55. We do not have to guess about the cause of his distress. He was facing the hatred and the oppression of enemies who wanted to take his life (vv. 2-4). When he wrote Psalm 57, he was up against the very same 'pelican problem' again. He says, 'My soul is among lions' (v. 4). These 'lions' were vicious men who had 'dug a pit'; in other words, they planned for his destruction.

David was, therefore, forced to deal with the very same question we are dealing with: how does a child of God cope with the 'pelican problem'? How is the believer to respond to great, overwhelming burdens?

The dove

The first thing that came to David's mind in Psalm 55 was to hide from it all. He, like the author of Psalm 102, was feeling very much like a pelican, but he longed for the wings of a dove so he could fly away and 'be at rest'. The dove is a very gentle, peaceful bird and is, therefore, a fitting emblem for one who is longing for peace.

Have you found yourself longing for the same thing? Have you ever found yourself wishing you could just fly away — away from your problems and your responsibilities?

David did not stay with that wishful thinking. He knew it was impossible. It did not take him long to adopt another strategy. He realized he did not need a set of wings for himself, because he had another set of wings that would serve him far better. He says to the Lord in the opening words of Psalm 57, 'And in the shadow of your wings I will make my refuge, until these calamities have passed by.' In other words, he did not need the wings of a dove because he had the wings of the mother hen. He did not need escaping wings because he had sheltering wings.

While he does not talk about the 'wings' of God in Psalm 55, it is clear that he had much the same thing in mind. He says, 'Cast your burden on the Lord, and he shall sustain you...'(v. 22).

Each time David faced 'the pelican problem', then, he found a sufficient resource in his God. And when the problems and burdens of life mount up around us to the point where we are reduced to 'pelican' living, we can find everything we need in our God. As he was sufficient for David, so he will be sufficient for us. We do not have to wish for wings to carry us away to a hiding-place. We already have in our God the wings we need. God himself is our hiding-place.

But how do we go about making God our hiding-place? How do we go about drawing sufficiency from our God when we are burdened and distressed?

The baby chicks

We can receive instruction from the little chicks that run to their mother for refuge. When danger arises, the mother hen clucks and spreads her wings, and the chicks run immediately under those wings and stay there until the danger is over.

There we have a perfect picture of what the distressed child of God is to do with his burden. He must heed the 'clucking' of God, deliberately and immediately run to the shelter of his 'wings', and stay there until the distress is gone.

Listening to the Word of God

How does this work out in practice? First, we must recognize the parallel between the hen's clucking and God's Word. The hen's clucking is at one and the same time a warning and a comfort to her chicks. It tells them danger is lurking, but it also tells them she will protect them.

God's Word is likewise a means of warning and comfort for the child of God. It tells him of the many dangers lurking about him. We don't like to hear this, but the truth is that much of our sense of being burdened can be explained in terms of problems we have brought on ourselves by ignoring the clear warnings of the Word of God.

The Word of God also comforts. It tells us to bring our burdens to the Lord. It tells us he cares and understands. It tells us his grace is more than sufficient for us and that he himself will never leave nor forsake us. It tells us that he will not allow the burdens of life to completely overwhelm us, but will sustain and strengthen us (Ps. 55:22).

Deliberately resorting to God

Secondly, we must recognize the parallel between the chick running to the mother hen and the saint of God deliberately resorting to God in times of trouble.

All the clucking in the world is of no avail if the chick refuses to run to the mother hen and get under her wings. And the cautioning, comforting clucking of God's Word is of no avail to the Christian if he refuses to act upon it by running to his God in the time of trial.

How does the child of God run to God? The psalms we have been looking at supply the answer. The Christian runs to God through prayer. David says, 'I will cry out to God Most High, to God who performs all things for me' (Ps. 57:2). He also says, 'As for me, I will call upon God, and the Lord shall save me (Ps. 55:16).

One of our hymns puts it like this:

What a friend we have in Jesus
All our sins and griefs to bear!
What a privilege to carry
Everything to God in prayer!

(Joseph Scriven)

The Christian also runs to God by running to praise (Ps. 57:7-11). David knew there was power in praise. Do we understand this? It works like this: the more absorbed we are with God, the less absorbed we shall be with our burdens and our cares.

Staying ourselves upon the Lord

Finally, there is a parallel between the chick staying under the mother's wings until the danger is past and the Christian staying himself upon God. David determined, not to run to God for a brief moment, and then dart away. He says, 'My heart is steadfast, O God, my heart is steadfast...' (Ps. 57:7).

There is all the difference in the world between giving God a try and making him our stay. Those who do the latter find strength to bear their burdens. What is it to make God our stay? It means to rest ourselves on him and his Word in every situation of life. When things are good we are stayed on God. When things fall apart, we are still stayed on God.

Stayed upon Jehovah
Hearts are fully blessed;
Finding as he promised,
Perfect peace and rest.

(Frances R. Havergal)

Have you felt like a pelican lately? The solution to the 'pelican problem', the problem of being so burdened that we feel utterly alone and desolate, is not in the wings of escape but in the sheltering 'wings' of our God. May God help us to understand this and to continually resort to our God in every situation of life.

23.
Asaph:
the trap of envying the wicked

Psalm 73

Here Asaph unfolds a dilemma that made his spirit droop to the point where he was almost completely overcome with despair (Ps. 73:2). What was it that packed such a punch that it almost floored Asaph? Let him answer: 'For I was envious of the boastful, when I saw the prosperity of the wicked' (v. 3).

The prosperity of the wicked

Have you ever been caught in that trap? Most Christians are forced to admit that they have. Here we are trying to live for the Lord and it seems as if we have difficulties, problems and burdens galore. All the while those around us have no concern at all for the things of God, and their lives appear to be as smooth as silk. They are loaded down with material possessions and they are always in robust health. Their cars never seem to break down, and their youngsters do not even need to wear glasses or braces on their teeth. Their lives are like their lawns, well-manicured with not so much as a single blade of grass out of place.

This is what staggered Asaph. He noted that the wicked 'are not in trouble as other men; nor are they plagued like other men' (v. 5). It seemed to Asaph that the wicked did not struggle in life. He says, 'They have more than heart could wish' (v. 7). And they did not even appear to struggle in death. Asaph notes that there were 'no pangs in their death; but their strength is firm' (v. 4). To Asaph's mind these wicked people who enjoyed such ease and luxury in life ought at least to have a hard death, but he was forced to admit that they seemed to die quite easily. Death was not unusually harsh or severe for them. So the wicked appeared to him to be blessed in life and death.

Perhaps most disconcerting to Asaph was the attitude of the wicked in all of this. One would at least expect them to realize how blessed they were and to show some sign of gratitude and a dash of humility. But such was not the case. They seemed to go about with no regard for their blessings and no concern for those around them who were not so blessed. Instead they went about brandishing pride as though it were a decorative chain worn around their necks (v. 6). Further, they did not hesitate to speak 'loftily' (v. 8). Instead of thanking God for the tranquillity and affluence they enjoyed, they 'set their mouth against the heavens' (v. 9).

In short, Asaph insists that the wicked people of his day were arrogant, violent and affluent. They appeared to regard themselves as richly deserving all they had, and they had not even the slightest sense of obligation to honour God or to help anyone else.

The difficulty of the righteous

After pondering the wicked, Asaph turned his attention to himself and others who were seeking to live righteously. And what he saw drove him even further into gloom and despair. He would no doubt have been satisfied if he had been able to see the people of God doing as well as the wicked. But they were nowhere near that level. Asaph's observation of God's people drove him to say that they were constantly drinking out of a full cup of affliction (v. 10). Asaph testified to his own share of affliction in these words: 'For all day long I have been plagued, and chastened every morning' (v. 14). Now here is affliction! Asaph says he had it all day and every day.

Caught in this vice of the prosperity of the wicked and the adversity of the righteous, Asaph finally gave way to this melancholy cry of despair: 'Surely I have cleansed my heart in vain, and washed my hands in innocence' (v. 13).

This is Asaph at his lowest point. His spirit had sagged, slipped and sunk to the very bottom. He and his fellow believers were so low that they had even begun to wonder if God was aware of their situation (v. 11).

The way of relief

We must not, however, leave Asaph with his sagging spirit. We must rather proceed to observe how he handled himself and how he worked himself out of this crushing dilemma.

What Asaph refrained from doing

We should notice in the first place that he restrained himself from infecting the people of God with his doubt and despair. He could have spoken openly about his state of mind, but he refused to do so. He says to the Lord, 'If I had said, "I will speak thus," behold, I would have been untrue to the generation of your children' (v. 15).

Asaph did by writing this psalm finally share his despair with all future generations of believers, but only after he had worked through it. He did not write it until then. We might say he refrained from writing when he had only the first fourteen verses to write. He took up his pen only when he had the last fourteen verses.

We can learn much from Asaph at this point. How quickly we vent our doubts and despair without giving so much as a single thought to the detrimental effect we may have upon others! Our first conclusions regarding our problems are seldom our best, and if we quickly share those initial conclusions we may do considerable harm to the faith of others.

What Asaph did

In addition to telling us what he restrained himself from doing, Asaph also tells us what he did. He says he 'went into the sanctuary of God' (v. 17). This was the decisive thing, the turning-point, in this crisis. There in the Lord's house Asaph found the handle for dealing with this problem. There, he tells us, he 'understood their end' (v. 17); that is, he came to understand the end of the wicked whom he had been envying.

The house of God

What was there about the house of God that brought Asaph to this insight? Was it the public reading of the Word of God? Was it the exposition of that Word? Was it something he heard in his conversation with other believers? It could have been one or more of these things. The important thing is that the answer came to him while he was engaged in the public worship of God.

What a resource believers have in the house of God! How often we have found, as Asaph did, that some feature of it spoke directly to the sadness and despair we were feeling, and we have gone away comforted and rejoicing! It is more than a little lamentable these days that so few of the people of God give evidence of realizing in any adequate measure what a wonderful resource public worship is. The sad fact is that when problems arise many Christians stop attending public worship. Ask them why and they lamely say something like this: 'I just don't feel like going' — as if we are exempt from keeping the commandments of the Lord if we do not feel like keeping them! Little do they realize that the very sadness and despair that keep them from wanting to attend the house of God can be treated there. It is no small irony that the very reason they plead for not attending public worship is one of the primary reasons why they should do so.

The author of Psalm 84 underscores the importance of public worship. He takes us to one of the most prominent features of Jewish life, a pilgrimage to the temple in Jerusalem. That temple was, of course, the centre of Jewish life. While the Jews understood that their God was so great that even 'the heaven of heavens' could not 'contain' him (1 Kings 8:27), they also realized that there was a sense in which he had been pleased to make the temple his dwelling-place.

This psalmist relates something of how he and the pilgrims travelling with him felt about worship at the temple. One of the things he stresses is the strength they received as they journeyed along. We would expect to read that with each passing day the pilgrims grew more and more weary until finally their strength was depleted. But just the opposite was the case. The closer the pilgrims came to the city, the stronger they became. Their love for worship was so great that the mere anticipation of it had an energizing effect upon them. This strength was so great that even the Valley of Baca, a particularly arid and barren valley through which they had to travel, did not bother them (Ps. 84:6).

How we need to let this picture sink into our hearts! We do not have to make long pilgrimages through treacherous terrain to reach the house of God. But it is not too fanciful to suggest that each week is something like a pilgrimage to the

Lord's house. During that pilgrimage we often find ourselves in the Valley of Baca. Our circumstances are difficult, and we often feel like weeping. But those who are faithful to worship God find that they have strength for traversing that valley. Drawing strength from the previous Sunday's worship and anticipating the next Sunday's worship, they go from 'strength to strength' (Ps. 84:7).

The end of the wicked

We must not leave Asaph finding balm and solace in the house of the Lord without noting the specific insight he fastened upon while there — that is, the end of the wicked. There in the Lord's house Asaph realized that he had made a colossal blunder. He had been content to look solely at the here and now. He had failed to consider all the facts. When he went to public worship he began to think in terms of eternity. (The house of the Lord does have a wonderful way of bringing the eternal to bear upon the temporal.)

As Asaph pondered the end of the wicked, he came to see that this is really the decisive thing. It is the end that makes the difference. It did not matter how happy and prosperous the wicked appeared to be in this life. The immensely important matter was what lay ahead of them. Asaph began to understand that, with all their carefree days and ways, the wicked were standing on a slippery slope and would ultimately be plunged into eternal destruction.

The Lord Jesus spoke of this same matter in terms of two ways, one broad and the other narrow (Matt. 7:13-14). Everyone must travel one of these two roads. The former is filled with travellers because it is a wide and easy road to travel. The latter, on the other hand, offers demanding and rigorous travel. At first glance the choice seems to be obvious. Why not take the easy way? It is so inviting and appealing, and there are so many who are travelling it. But the wise traveller is concerned about one thing, and one thing alone. It does not matter how easy one road is and how difficult the other. The only thing that really counts is where these roads lead. And the Lord Jesus left no doubt about this at all. That broad road, he said, leads to eternal destruction, while the narrow road leads to life. All is very different now! If that broad road leads only to eternal ruin, it does not matter how pleasant the journey is; and if that narrow road leads to eternal bliss, it does not matter how many hardships there are along the way. All that matters is the destination.

When Asaph reflected on these things he was amazed that he could have been so foolish (Ps. 73:22), and he exulted in the God who held him by his right hand (v. 23) and would some day lead him into glory (v. 24). If we will join Asaph in his reflections we shall share his conclusions. We shall see how foolish it is to envy anyone who is heading for eternal destruction, no matter how wonderful his life appears to be. And we shall be filled with praise and wonder that we have, by the grace of God, been placed on the road to eternal life, no matter how hard and difficult our circumstances may be.

24.
The man of God from Judah: subjective experience and the Word of God

1 Kings 13:1-26

The wickedness of King Jeroboam of Israel gives us yet another opportunity to observe a danger that constantly threatens the people of God, namely, that of putting subjective experiences above the Word of God. We may do this with our own experiences or with those of someone else.

The unnamed prophet of 1 Kings 13 gives us insight into this tragedy. This prophet was sent by the Lord from Judah to publicly denounce the new religion that Jeroboam had established in the kingdom of Israel. This religion, as we have previously noted, centred around the worship of a golden calf (1 Kings 12:28-29).

A clearly defined task

It is essential that we understand that there was absolutely no ambiguity in the assignment that the Lord gave his prophet. The prophet was to go to Bethel (1 Kings 13:1), speak out publicly against Jeroboam's idolatrous altar (v. 2), give a sign to confirm his message (v. 3) and return home by another way without pausing to eat or drink (v. 9).

An admirable performance

As the chapter unfolds we find the prophet performing his task in a very admirable and wonderful way. He went to Bethel, found Jeroboam at the altar preparing to burn incense to his calf and publicly proclaimed concerning that altar: 'O altar, altar! Thus says the Lord: "Behold, a child, Josiah by name, shall be born to the house of David; and on you he shall sacrifice the priests of the high places who burn incense on you, and men's bones shall be burned on you" ' (v. 2). He then announced the confirming sign that the Lord had given him — namely, that the altar would split apart and its ashes would pour out (v. 3).

Jeroboam did not, of course, take kindly to this. After hearing the prophet's sign, he pointed towards him and gave the order: 'Arrest him!' (v. 4). No sooner were the words out of his mouth than he received an unexpected confirmation of the truth of the prophet's message. His hand 'withered' so that he could not pull it back (v. 4), and the altar split apart, just as the prophet had said (v. 5).

The withering of his hand and the splitting apart of the altar caused Jeroboam to have a very quick change of heart about this prophet. He knew now that he was indeed in the presence of a true prophet of the living God, and he begged the prophet to pray for the healing of his hand. The prophet did so, and Jeroboam's hand was restored as quickly as it had been afflicted (v. 6).

Jeroboam even went so far as to invite the prophet to his home, but the prophet refused by categorically stating what the Lord had said to him: 'You shall not eat bread, nor drink water, nor return by the same way you came' (v. 9). And he set off on a route different from the one by which he came, just as the Lord had commanded him (v. 10).

It was in every respect a very dazzling performance, and we would have expected the story to now come to an end by reading that the prophet returned to Judah and lived happily ever after.

An unexpected twist

But suddenly a new and totally unexpected dimension enters the picture in the form of an old prophet. Two words ought to make us very suspicious of this old fellow: the words 'prophet' and 'Bethel'. He, a prophet, lived right at the very centre of Jeroboam's religion, but we do not read that he ever spoke out against Jeroboam or his altar. He appears to have been quite happy to go along in peaceful co-existence with Jeroboam's religion while perhaps regaling himself with memories of former strong stands for God and truth.

This old man's truce with the false religion of Jeroboam was shattered when he received from his sons an account of what the prophet from Judah had done (v. 11). The sterling performance of the prophet from Judah and the way that performance excited his sons shamed him, but instead of quietly seeking a place of repentance, the old prophet went after his fellow-prophet (vv. 12-14).

Why did he do this? If he could persuade the prophet from Judah to come and spend some time with him, it would look as if the two were equal, and his own failure to speak out against Jeroboam's idolatry would be covered, or at least lessened in the eyes of his sons.

So desperate was the old man to have the respectability conferred by the presence of his fellow-prophet that he resorted to deceit to achieve it. He overcame the prophet's refusal to dine with him by assuring him that he had received a visit from an angel of the Lord. He claimed that this angel had assured him that it would be quite all right for the prophet of Judah to eat and drink in Bethel after all, that his earlier orders had been revoked (v. 18).

The prophet of Judah believed this word and went home with the old man. He trusted in what he believed to be a valid experience rather than in the Word of God. It does not matter that the old prophet had not actually had this experience but only fabricated it. The point is that the prophet of Judah accepted this man's claim at face value and put his faith in the subjective experience of the old prophet.

To the argument that all the prophets of God received their messages only through subjective experience, we may respond that the prophet of Judah had by this point moved into another realm. He had seen God honour his obedience to the word he had originally received, that word which plainly called him to return home without stopping to eat or drink. Although the prophet of Judah had distinct confirmation that his message was indeed from God, he refused to trust that word all the way through. Instead he subjugated what he knew to be the word of God to a subjective experience.

A tragic end

The prophet from Judah did not realize his folly until he was actually sitting at the old prophet's table. There his host suddenly announced that the man of God would not return home but would die because of his disobedience to God (vv. 20-22). That prophecy was tragically fulfilled. As the prophet from Judah made his way home, he was met by a lion and killed (vv. 23-24).

An abiding truth

This strange account forcefully proclaims a truth that is much needed by the church today. This truth may be put in these words: we must never put subjective experiences, whether they be our own or another's, above the Word of God. We have God's Word in Scripture. The apostle Paul firmly declares: 'All Scripture is given by inspiration of God, and is profitable for doctrine, for reproof, for correction, for instruction in righteousness, that the man of God may be complete, thoroughly equipped for every good work' (2 Tim. 3:16-17).

The apostle Peter explains Scripture in this way: 'Holy men of God spoke as they were moved by the Holy Spirit' (2 Peter 1:21).

It is very significant that Peter makes this statement shortly after referring to an indescribably glorious experience of his own, one in which he saw the Lord Jesus take on a heavenly appearance before his very eyes. Peter says that he and those with him were 'eyewitnesses of his majesty' (2 Peter 1:16). He then adds: 'For he received from God the Father honour and glory when such a voice came to him from the excellent glory: "This is my beloved Son, in whom I am well pleased." And we heard this voice which came from heaven when we were with him on the holy mountain' (vv. 17-18).

What a remarkable experience! But the apostle Peter proceeds to say that he and the other disciples had something even more sure than that experience. What was that more sure thing? It was the Word of God! Peter placed the Word of God above his own experience. He would readily have argued, as the apostle John did, that the fact that we have an experience does not necessarily mean it came from God because many false prophets are in this world (1 John 4:1). It is essential, therefore, that we check our experiences against the teachings of God's Word.

This runs counter to much of Christendom today. Nothing is more common among today's Christians than placing personal experiences above Scripture. Sometimes it is put very bluntly. One believer went so far as to write in the flyleaf of his

Bible: 'I don't care what the Bible says; I've had an experience.'[1]

The same mentality is evident in this popular slogan: 'The man with experience is never at the mercy of a man with an argument.'

Subjective experiences are widely considered by today's Christians to be self-authenticating. As far as they are concerned, a moving experience is beyond dispute. Anything they have experienced must of necessity be true. If someone has had an experience, he or she can rely on that. It could not possibly be wrong.

The false prophets of Jeremiah's day were placing their experiences above the Word of God. Each one was going about saying, 'I have dreamed, I have dreamed!' (Jer. 23:25). God was not impressed with these prophets and their dreams. Jeremiah records his response to them in these words:

'The prophet who has a dream, let him tell a dream;
And he who has my word, let him speak my word faith-
   fully.
What is the chaff to the wheat?' says the Lord
                                        (Jer. 23:28).

God made, then, a clear distinction between his Word and the emotional experiences of the false prophets. He tells them not to equate the two and not to in any way pass their experiences off as being equal to, or superior to, his Word. The two were no more equal than chaff is equal to grain.

No one put this truth in a more devastating and dramatic way than the apostle Paul did in his letter to the Galatian Christians. Paul urged them not to move away from the gospel of Jesus Christ, no matter if the temptation came from an angel of heaven. The apostle says, 'But even if we, or an angel from heaven, preach any other gospel to you than what we have preached to you, let him be accursed' (Gal. 1:8).

Subjective experiences can be very appealing and moving, but they cannot compare with the Word of God and must not be placed above it. The prophet from Judah for ever testifies to this abiding truth.

25.
Hezekiah: dealing with moral filth

2 Chronicles 29:3-5,15-16

We all know how easy it is for things to get dirty. Houses get dirty. So do cars, children, pets and our own bodies. A lot of our time and energy is taken up with cleaning dirty things.

Are you aware that there are different kinds of dirt? There is the type of dirt that I have been talking about, physical dirt. But there is also moral dirt. Have you ever heard someone say something was 'common as dirt'? I do not hesitate to suggest that moral dirt is as common as the physical dirt on which we walk. This kind of dirt gets into our individual hearts and minds. It gets into our homes. It gets into our churches and into our nation.

Moral dirt not only gets into these things, but it finally ruins them. It has the same effect that sand would have if it were poured into the gears of a machine. The good news is this: moral dirt can be dealt with.

When Hezekiah came to the throne of the nation of Judah, he found it was in need of a good spiritual and moral scrubbing. The chapter before us tells us about that scrubbing. As we analyse it, we can learn how to get the moral dirt out of our own lives.

We need to consult this chapter and let it speak to us. The truth is that many of us need a good, old-fashioned spiritual scrubbing. We need to have our spiritual ears scrubbed so we can hear what God is saying to us. We need to get the filth and dirt off our spiritual hands. We need to have our spiritual feet soaked. We need our spiritual eyes flushed out so we can see again. Some of us need our mouths washed out with spiritual soap.

We don't like to hear such things. It is far easier to be concerned about the filth in our churches and in our nation than about that which is in our own lives. We need to understand that the churches and the nation are merely extensions of ourselves. When individuals are scrubbed clean, the churches and the nation will be changed. How, then, do we go about this business of spiritual scrubbing?

The danger of moral filth

First, there must be a bedrock conviction that moral dirt is extremely dangerous and harmful. When Hezekiah came to the throne of Judah it was obvious that the nation was in a state of deep distress. Enemies had been menacing the nation's existence (2 Chron. 28:16-18,20), many of the citizens had either been killed or deported (2 Chron. 29:9) and the temple of the Lord had been shut down (v. 7).

Some of Hezekiah's subjects may have been in doubt about the reason for the nation's distress, but Hezekiah was not. He put his finger squarely on the problem: 'Therefore the wrath of the Lord fell upon Judah and Jerusalem, and he has given them up to trouble, to desolation, and to jeering, as you see with your eyes' (v. 8).

Hezekiah could see something we seem to have trouble seeing — rebellion against the Lord is no small, innocuous thing. It sets the stage for horrific damage and distress. It does so because God is firmly and unalterably opposed to it. Sin in the lives of his people stirs him to take action to bring them to their senses.

We shall never be inclined to address the moral filth that
has crept into our lives until we begin with the conviction that
moral filth is doing us great harm and must be dealt with.

Moral filth requires a diligent approach

That brings us to a second principle, which is that dealing with
moral filth requires diligent effort.

How diligent and persistent Hezekiah was in this matter of
spiritually scrubbing his nation! He started with the spiritual
leaders (v. 4). First, they were to 'sanctify' themselves (v. 5).
That means they were to dedicate themselves to the business
of a spiritual renewal.

These men were in desperate need of such a renewal. They
had stood by while Hezekiah's father, Ahaz, had closed the
temple and gone after idols. Perhaps we think they had no
choice. Ahaz was, after all, their king. These men had, however, been charged by a far greater King than Ahaz, the Lord
himself, to maintain the worship of the temple. In not standing
up to Ahaz, they had demonstrated their willingness to obey
men rather than God.

Hezekiah's command for them to sanctify themselves was,
therefore, a clarion call for them to repent of their neglect,
return in their hearts to the Lord and renew their covenant
with him.

The dirt of neglect

These men heeded Hezekiah's call. They opened up the temple.
What a sight greeted them! The dirt of neglect was there.
Matthew Henry calls this 'the common dirt it had contracted
while it was shut up — dust, and cobwebs, and the rust of the
vessels'.[1]

The dirt of the outside world

In addition, there was dirt that had been tracked in, the pollution that had been carried in from the outside world, represented by the idols and the idolatrous altar that Ahaz had brought into the temple (2 Kings 16:10-16). Matthew Henry says this altar, 'though kept ever so neat', was 'a greater pollution' to the house of God 'than if it had been made the common sewer of the city'.[2]

Hidden dirt

There was also hidden dirt. Verse 16 tells us the priests went into 'the inner part of the house of the Lord to cleanse it'.

No one apart from the priests was allowed to see this part of the temple. They could have been content merely to clean the part that the public saw and have left this hidden part alone, but they realized that this part which was so far from the eyes of men was not hidden from the eyes of God.

Their first look at all the dirt and filth in the temple must have been quite overwhelming for these men, but they tackled it just the same, and sixteen days later the job was complete (2 Chron. 29:16).

It was a massive job that yielded only to diligent effort, and these men gave it the diligence it required.

The dirt of our lives

Has it occurred to you that we have in this account a very accurate and disturbing picture of ourselves? Do we not see the same kind of dirt in our lives as the priests and Levites found in the temple? Is it not true that many of us are coated with the dirt of neglect? Our Bibles often have dust on them. Our prayer closets often have cobwebs in them. Our relationships with our fellow-Christians are all too often rusty and unsightly.

Is it not true that we also have a lot of dirt in our lives that has been tracked in from outside? How often we take our cue for what we should think and how we should act from the world around us and from the latest opinion poll rather than from the Word of God!

And what about that hidden dirt? We may appear clean and upright before men, but what does God see? What unclean desires and thoughts do we carry around with us?

If we want to avoid the calamitous damage of sin and bring the blessing of God on our lives, we must tackle sin in all its forms. It is not easy work. It requires us to stop justifying and excusing ourselves and to repent before God. It may require us to go to a brother or sister in Christ to seek forgiveness and to make restitution. But, difficult and demanding as the work is, it must be done if we are to have spiritual renewal.

Moral filth calls for a thorough approach

Yet another principle for removing moral dirt is apparent in these verses. It may be put in this way: removing moral filth requires a thorough and extensive effort.

The priests brought out 'all the debris' (v. 16), cleansed 'all the house' (v. 18) and the altar of the Lord 'with all its articles' (v. 18), and the table of showbread 'with all its articles' (v. 18). They also brought back into the temple 'all the articles' which Ahaz had cast aside (v. 19)

What did they do with all the rubbish and debris they found in the temple? They carried it to the Brook Kidron. This is very significant. The Kidron Valley ran from an area north of Jerusalem past the temple and the Mt of Olives to the Dead Sea. For most of the year that valley was a dry river-bed, but in the rainy season it became a torrent. It was a perfect place for the people of Jerusalem to dump their rubbish because when that rainy season came all that rubbish would be entirely swept away to the Dead Sea. The Brook Kidron may be said, therefore, to represent a total removal, or complete clean-up.

Let us learn from this the importance of rejecting half measures as we go after the rubbish in our lives. We shall never be perfect in this life, but let us make sure that we declare war on all our sins and do not declare a truce with one or two. Only then do we have the right to expect a true revival.

We must not leave this passage without noting something else about this renewal in which Hezekiah led — that is, the joy that was produced by it (2 Chron. 29:30,36; 30:26-27).

Satan has been very effective in spreading a colossal lie. He has succeeded in creating the impression that sin brings us joy and the commandments of God bring us misery and woe. Just the opposite is true. Sin brings nothing but heartache and ruin, and the commandments of God bring abounding happiness.

We should not need to be told this. All we have to do is look around us. For many years our society has been going deeper and deeper into sin, and all we have to show for it is heartache. Isn't it time for us to acknowledge candidly the hurtfulness of sin and to turn to God with a diligent and thorough attack upon our sins? Isn't it time for us to stop neglecting the things of God and to throw out the dirt that has been tracked in and all the hidden dirt in our lives? May God help us to do so and to find the joy that comes from dealing with the threat posed by moral filth.

26.
Daniel: resisting conformity with the world's values

Daniel 1:1-16

The Babylonians carried Daniel and his friends away from their homes in Jerusalem and settled them in Babylon. The Babylonians were not satisfied merely to deprive these young men of their homeland. They were set on getting Daniel and his friends to repudiate their Jewish values in favour of embracing the values of Babylon.

The source of Daniel's values

As far as the Babylonians were concerned, it should not have been a big deal to replace one set of values with another. Daniel and his friends were not in Jerusalem now but in Babylon and they should, therefore, do as the Babylonians did. But Daniel and his friends saw the situation in an entirely different light. They understood that their Jewish values and the Babylonian values were not equal and interchangeable. The former had not just evolved over a period of time. They had been given to the nation by God himself.

The very existence of the Jews was due to God. It was God who called the father of the nation, Abraham. It was God who had preserved Abraham's descendants while they were enslaved in Egypt and finally delivered them from Egypt. It was God who constituted them as a nation under the law of Moses. It was God who had brought them into the land of Canaan and established them there. All of this and much more indicated that the Jews were no ordinary people. They were God's own special possession.

The fact that Daniel and his friends now found themselves in Babylon did not mean they could just throw all this out of the window. They understood that their very presence in Babylon testified to the reality of their God and his faithfulness to keep his word. God had warned his people to stay away from idols and had pledged to send them away into captivity if they refused to heed his warning. They had refused and the captivity had come as God had said it would.

Daniel and his friends came to Babylon, then, with the burning realization that God's people had better obey him. They came there with the understanding that they were going to be a distinct minority in a culture that was largely hostile to their beliefs. They came there with a pointed question constantly throbbing in their minds: how could they live in this new culture without being absorbed by it?

The test of Daniel's values

They were no sooner there than they were tempted at this point of obedience to God. They were enrolled in a special school that would train them to serve the king (Dan. 1:5), and Babylonian food was placed before them. There were, of course, some parts of the Babylonian culture that did not conflict with the things of God, and at those points Daniel and his friends did not hesitate to conform (they accepted Babylonian names and were ready to accept Babylonian jobs). But at those points at which Babylonian culture flew in the face of the law of God, Daniel and his friends were called upon to stand for God. And this food, although it seemed so innocent and harmless, was one of those points.

The pressure to yield at this point was intense. Political pressure, the chance to move ahead of the other young men, was there. Peer pressure, the pressure to do what everyone was doing, was there. Religious pressure was also there. The fact that Daniel and his friends were in captivity seemed to indicate that their God had failed and the gods of the Babylonians had prevailed. Why not, in the light of this, renounce their God and go along with the worship of the Babylonian gods?

The purpose of Daniel's heart

Although the pressure was enormous, Daniel and his friends refused to yield. How did they manage to resist such enormous pressure? The answer is given in these words: 'Daniel purposed in his heart that he would not defile himself...' (v. 8). Does this mean that Daniel was one of those rare men who was able, through iron will and steadfast determination, to carry out what he resolved to do?

There can be no doubt that determination to carry out his resolve was present, but there is more than that here. Daniel's resolve was fed by something else. It was the realization that he was not in the final analysis a citizen of the kingdom of Babylon, or the kingdom of Judah, but rather of a far greater kingdom — the kingdom of heaven. And his sovereign was not Nebuchadnezzar or any other earthly ruler, but rather 'the God of heaven' (Dan. 2:18,19,28,37,44). Daniel spoke to his friends of this God in this way:

> ... wisdom and might are his.
> And he changes the times and the seasons;
> He removes kings and raises up kings;
> He gives wisdom to the wise
> And knowledge to those who have understanding.

He reveals deep and secret things;
He knows what is in the darkness,
And light dwells with him

(Dan. 2:20-22).

Realizing there is such a God in heaven changes everything here on earth. Such a God can be trusted to protect and vindicate his people when they take a stand for him. Trust is exactly what Daniel and his friends did. They requested that they be given ten days to go without the king's food, and then be judged as to whether they were better off than those who ate of the king's food (Dan. 1:11-13). And the God of heaven saw to it that they were better off (v. 15).

The lessons from Daniel's life

It should be obvious to all of us who know the Lord that we are in a situation very similar to the one in which Daniel and his friends found themselves. We are also a minority group within a culture that is often hostile to the things of God. The question we have to face is the same as the one confronting those men: how do we live in this culture without being eaten up by it?

Many professing Christians seem to have answered the question by caving in at every point. They uncritically accept all that our own modern-day Babylon has to offer. They think like the Babylonians, talk like them and act like them. Everything about them is more Babylonian than it is Christian.

But merely calling oneself a Christian does not make one so, and those who have comfortably settled in with the Babylonians only show their true colours.

It is impossible for Christians to be completely at ease in a world such as this. For them the age-old question remains: how does one live as a Christian in a Babylonian world?

The ability to stay true to God in our own Babylon comes only as we purpose in our hearts to be true, and we can only purpose that in our hearts if we take a long and ruthless look at the competing kingdoms.

Take a look at Babylon. Yes, there is much about it that is attractive and appealing, things which God's people are free to enjoy when they do not conflict with the Word of God, but with all its attractiveness and appeal, the kingdom of Babylon is a kingdom only of this world and will finally pass away.

Then take a look at the kingdom of God. That kingdom offers beauties and glories that make the beauties of this world seem dull and dim, and that kingdom endures for ever. Nebuchadnezzar, King of Babylon, was finally compelled to acknowledge this truth. He says of the Lord: 'His dominion is an everlasting dominion, and his kingdom is from generation to generation' (Dan. 4:34).

We shall never be able to stand in our own Babylon until we realize that we are citizens of a far greater kingdom, a kingdom that will never pass away. And the God of that kingdom can be trusted to strengthen and help us even in the face of enormous pressure.

How do we know there is such a kingdom? Is it just a figment of our imagination, a mere will-o'-the-wisp, a product of wishful thinking? No, thank God, it is far more certain than that. We know beyond any shadow of doubt that there is such a kingdom because one came from there, lived among us, died for us, arose from the grave and returned to heaven. This one is none other than the Lord Jesus Christ. And when we stop to ponder who he is and what he has done for us, we not only realize the reality of the kingdom of heaven, but we most certainly find ourselves desiring to live in this Babylon in a way that brings glory to him.

27.
Jonah: a warning against running from God

Jonah 1:1-3,17

I remember running a lot as a child. Often I would run to perform some chore on the farm. My brother and I would run when we were going fishing or when we were off to play baseball. Sometimes I ran just out of the sheer joy of being young and energetic.

It occurred to me some years ago that I had stopped running. I don't know exactly when it happened. I just realized one day that I was running only on very rare occasions. Even now as I think about it I can only remember running once in recent years, and that was to catch a plane in Charlotte, North Carolina. And then I thought my lungs would burst. A sadness creeps over me when I realize that my days of running are over.

The Christian life consists of both walking and running. There are some parts of it that require steady, consistent effort. That is the walking part. But there are other parts of it that require speedy, diligent effort. That is the running part. We are to walk in communion with the Lord, but we are to run in service to our Lord and in obedience to his commands.

I wonder if you have done a running inventory lately? Such an inventory would cause many Christians to admit that they have virtually stopped running. There is a sadness about a Christian who was once eager to run in service and obedience but has now slowed to a snail's pace. Is there anything sadder than a Christian who does not run any more?

As I thought about this matter of spiritual running, I found my mind drawn inexorably to the prophet Jonah.

It is the job of a prophet to run swiftly with the Word of God. And Jonah evidently ran well on previous occasions. God would say to his prophet, 'Go over there,' and Jonah would run. God would speak again: 'Jonah, go over there,' and Jonah would run.

But then one day God said, 'Jonah, go to Nineveh,' and this prophet who had run so well on previous occasions did not run. Well, he ran, but not towards Nineveh. This little book that bears his name says, 'But Jonah arose to flee to Tarshish from the presence of the Lord. He went down to Joppa, and found a ship going to Tarshish; so he paid the fare, and went down into it, to go with them to Tarshish from the presence of the Lord' (Jonah 1:3). So to be perfectly accurate we have to say that Jonah did not stop running altogether. He stopped running for God and began to run away from him.

Three truths come to mind as I review the familiar details of Jonah's running from the Lord. These are truths that pertain only to those who are children of God.

Running from God's commandments equals running from God

The command from God to Jonah could not have been clearer: 'Arise, go to Nineveh...' (Jonah 1: 2). But Jonah refused to go. Yes, he had a reason. He did not want to preach to the Ninevites because he did not much care for them. They were enemies of his own people, and Jonah knew his preaching would probably bring them to repentance and that God would then lift his threatened judgement from them. Jonah did not want that judgement lifted. He wanted the Ninevites eliminated.

But whether he liked it or not, it was his responsibility to go. God's command made it his responsibility. When Jonah ran from that command, he ran from his responsibility, and when he ran from his responsibility he ran away from the presence of the Lord.

We live in strange days. Many Christians think nothing of throwing down their responsibilities at the drop of a hat. And yet if they were asked whether they are close to God they would quickly insist that they are. They believe it is possible to be in fellowship with God while ignoring his commands.

But this is a modern invention. The Bible assures us that when we run from the responsibilities God has given us, we simultaneously run from the presence of the Lord. Our fellowship with God is tied to our obedience to him. We cannot be close to him while we are running from his commands.

It is very important for us to be clear on this matter. We have a tendency to conclude that we are close to God if we have certain warm, fuzzy feelings, but God does not leave us to define for ourselves what constitutes closeness to him. He defines it for us, and his definition includes obedience to his commands. The Lord Jesus underscored the importance of obedience in these powerful words: 'But why do you call me "Lord, Lord," and not do the things which I say?' (Luke 6:46).

A second truth we can glean from Jonah's running from God may be put in the following way.

Running from God does not equal escaping

O. Palmer Robertson summarizes the message of this first chapter of Jonah in these words: 'Jonah is in flight. But God is in pursuit. It is a futile flight and it is a persistent pursuit.'[1]

In a sense, then, Jonah ran from God. But in another sense he did not. He could not. David stated this truth in one of his psalms:

Where can I go from your Spirit?
Or where can I flee from your presence? ...
Indeed, the darkness shall not hide from you,
But the night shines as the day;
The darkness and the light are both alike to you
                                              (Ps. 139:7,12).

Robertson states the same truth in these words: 'Trying to get away from God is like trying to get away from air.'[2]

What did the Lord do to bring back his running prophet? Two cryptic phrases tell the story. First we read, 'But the Lord sent out a great wind on the sea...' (Jonah 1:4). A little later we read, 'Now the Lord had prepared a great fish...' (v. 17).

The great wind achieved one end. It caused the sailors to throw Jonah into the sea (vv. 10-15). The fish, which had been awaiting Jonah's arrival in the sea, swallowed him whole and, in so doing, achieved another end, which was to cause Jonah to come to his senses and to repent (Jonah 2:1-10).

Jonah had run, but he had not escaped. The God from whom he ran chased him down and brought him into that position of obedience that Jonah had first refused to occupy. Jonah had fought with God, and God won. We are not surprised, therefore, to find Jonah dutifully making his way to Nineveh after the fish vomited him out onto the ground (Jonah 2:10 - 3:4).

The inescapable truth here is this: if we truly belong to God, he will never let us go. He will pursue us into our disobedience and our waywardness and eventually bring us back unto himself. We may rest assured that Paul's words are true: 'He who has begun a good work in you will complete it until the day of Jesus Christ' (Phil. 1:6).

We have another example of this truth in the pages of the New Testament. There we find Simon Peter straying dreadfully as he denies the Lord Jesus, not once, not twice, but three times. The Lord would certainly have been justified in washing his hands of Simon Peter once and for all. But he refused to do so. Instead he pursued him and brought him back into fellowship with himself and into usefulness for his kingdom (John 21).

Never underestimate the Lord in this business. He has many, many ways of bringing his children back. He can woo them gently and tenderly through the preaching and teaching of his Word. He can sternly warn and rebuke through that same Word. He can provide counsel and encouragement through Christian family members and friends.

And he can still send great storms and great fish. No, I am not suggesting that disobedience will cause a Christian to be thrown into the sea and be swallowed by a fish in the same way that Jonah was. That storm and that fish were simply the means God selected to chastise Jonah. God changes the means, but he still chastises his disobedient children (Heb. 12:5-11). The sombre truth of the matter is that if we who belong to the Lord run from him long enough, we shall most certainly run into trouble head-on.

As we think about the race that is set before us, it will do us good always to remember Jonah, and keep running. But we should also look beyond the negative example set by Jonah to the positive example of our Lord Jesus Christ. He also had a race set before him. His spiritual race began in glory and led through Bethlehem, Nazareth and the cities and villages of Palestine. The finishing-line was on a hill outside Jerusalem. There the Lord Jesus Christ gave up his life on a cruel Roman cross and in doing so purchased eternal salvation for all who believe. Had he stopped short in his race, there would be no salvation for any of us. But he did not stop short. There on Calvary's cross we see him crossing the finishing-line as he cries out: 'It is finished!' (John 19:30).

We can only run our race by 'looking unto Jesus, the author and finisher of our faith, who for the joy that was set before him endured the cross, despising the shame, and has sat down at the right hand of the throne of God' (Heb. 12:2).

28.
Malachi: a warning against unfaithfulness

Malachi 2:10-16

Malachi was one of the post-exilic prophets. He ministered to the people of God after their return from captivity in Babylon. By the time Malachi came on the scene, the people had been back in their homeland for a good long while. The temple had been rebuilt and the sacrifices had been resumed.

But all was not well. Miles Bennett describes the situation in this way: 'A spirit of dull depression had settled over the inhabitants of Jerusalem; scepticism and spiritual indifference held the people in their grasp.'[1]

God's antidote for his people was to send Malachi to carry on a dialogue with them. There are seven occurrences of dialogue in this short prophecy. Each of the seven consists of God making an accusation, the people raising an objection and God refuting the objection. These seven instances of dialogue are signalled by the words, 'you say' (Mal. 1:2,7,12-13; 2:14,17; 3:7,13).

The dialogue in the passage which forms the subject of this chapter is about loss, terrible loss. It gives us the sad account of the people coming to the altar of the Lord with tears streaming down their cheeks, only to have the Lord turn away from them in displeasure (Mal. 2:13).

What was going on here? We have a tendency to think that just going to the house of God ought to be enough in and of itself to please God, but these people were doing more than that. They were actually showing emotion while they were there. But God was not impressed with either their presence or their emotion.

Through his prophet, the Lord puts his finger on the reason why he was rejecting their religious efforts. The Lord accuses them of dealing 'treacherously'. That word appears five times in verses 10-16. It means 'deceitfully'. It is the opposite of acting with integrity or with dependability.

Three major truths emerge from this passage and call for our attention.

The major manifestation of unfaithfulness

First, we can see here the major manifestation of this treacherous dealing. We may be sure that this treacherous dealing ran through every part of their society, but there was one manifestation of it that was particularly unsavoury to the Lord. The prophet calls it an 'abomination' that 'profaned' the Lord's institution (v. 11).

He then proceeds to identify this abomination. He says the nation 'has married the daughter of a foreign god' (v. 11). A few verses later the prophet says the men of the nation have dealt treacherously with the wives of their youth (v. 14).

Evidently the men of Israel were now divorcing their elderly Jewish wives in order to marry younger and more attractive women from surrounding nations. This practice had become so extensive that the prophet could legitimately say that the whole nation of Judah had 'profaned' the Lord's institution. What was Malachi saying? The Lord's institution was his covenant relationship with his people, whom he loved, and that relationship was now being contaminated by the men of the nation treating their marriages so casually.

We may be inclined to think what goes on in our homes has no bearing on the rest of life. But it does. Here in Malachi's day we find men going to meet the Lord at church and the Lord points them back to their homes. Family life colours and influences every other part of life.

The appalling nature of unfaithfulness

That brings us to consider the appalling nature of this treacherous dealing.

Malachi wanted his people to understand that the sin the Lord was charging them with was no small thing. Satan adopts the opposite strategy. He first entices us by telling us that the course of action he is proposing is not sinful. When conscience protests that it is, he then assures us that even though it is sinful, it really does not matter all that much.

Malachi underscored the seriousness of what the men of Judah were doing by stressing three items of monumental importance.

The solidarity of the people of God

First, he stressed the solidarity of the people of God. He begins his discussion of this matter with some searching and probing questions:

Have we not all one Father?
Has not one God created us?
Why do we deal treacherously with one another
By profaning the covenant of the fathers?

(Mal. 2:10).

The men who were guilty of treacherous dealing with their wives would undoubtedly have been quick to insist that their actions affected no one but themselves. But Malachi would have none of it. The people were not only in covenant with God but with each other, and every act of unfaithfulness to God weakens and erodes the people of God as a whole.

The sacredness of marriage

Malachi also stressed the appalling nature of their sin by pointing out the sacredness of marriage. Marriage is not simply a social arrangement constructed by men. It is the design of God himself.

Malachi plainly says that God not only designed marriage, but he also designed it in a certain way. He calls attention to the fact that at the beginning God created only one companion for Adam. He could, of course, have created many women. Malachi says God had 'a remnant of the Spirit' (v. 15). In other words, God's creative acts in no way diminished his power or ability. After he created he still had plenty of power to create more. And after he took Eve from Adam's side, God's power was in no way depleted or expended. He could have made many wives for Adam. But in making Eve alone, God was making it clear that his design for marriage was for a man to have one wife.

There is, however, another dimension to this matter of oneness. God not only intended that each man should have one wife, but he also intended the two of them to be one. There is a physical oneness, but it goes beyond that. Oneness in marriage sometimes reaches such proportions that husbands and wives know what the other is thinking and often complete each other's sentences. True oneness is physical, emotional and spiritual.

Now we are in a position to understand why the next verse
refers to divorce as a violent act (v. 16). It rips one person
into two.

The potential for harm

Finally, Malachi stressed the seriousness of treacherous dealing in marriage by calling attention to its potential for harm.

Malachi makes it clear that disregard for the laws of God
can bring harm to the one who is guilty of it. He knows that
the Lord can and does chastise his people for sinful living, and
he even desires this to happen. He prays: 'May the Lord cut
off from the tents of Jacob the man who does this...' (v. 12).
This may seem to be a harsh thing to say, but Malachi would
rather see the Lord punish the men who were dealing treacherously than that the whole nation should suffer.

Another harmful effect of this faithless dealing had to do
with the children involved. Why did God want his people to
be faithful to their marriages? Malachi's answer is this: 'He
seeks godly offspring' (v. 15).

God himself is faithful, and he desires that we should be
faithful as well. One of the ways we learn faithfulness is by
seeing it at work in the home. If God had designed marriage in
such a way that a man would not have to be faithful to one
woman, the offspring of that marriage would not learn
faithfulness.

Joyce Baldwin writes, 'Only when both parents remain faithful to their marriage vows can the children be given the security which provides the basis for godly living. The family was
intended to be the school in which God's way of life was practised and learned...'[2]

All of these things make treacherous dealing in marriage a
very serious and weighty thing indeed. Thank God, we don't

have to leave it there. Malachi also gives us the remedy for treacherous dealing.

The remedy for unfaithfulness

Twice in these verses the prophet tells the men of his day to 'take heed' to their spirits (vv. 15,16). They had a clear and distinct law from God regarding marriage. Now the question before these men was what they would do about that law? Would they resent it and fly in the face of it? Or would they submit to it?

No words could be more vital for us. We know what God wants from our homes. We know he wants husbands and wives to be faithful to each other. We know that he wants us to practise Christian kindness and courtesy in our homes. We know that he wants us to rear our children to love and serve him.

But we live in a culture that ridicules and scorns these things and, if we are not careful, we can become so enamoured and infatuated with our culture that we find ourselves resenting the commands of God and adopting the standards of our society. Take heed, child of God, that you do not develop a resentful spirit towards the teachings of God's Word!

The prophet Amos spoke of God having a plumb-line for his people (Amos 7:7-8). The plumb-line was a device used by builders to determine if a wall was straight. It was a small, heavy weight attached to a cord and suspended to indicate a vertical line. Amos used the plumb-line to tell the people of Israel that God was looking at their lives to see if they were straight. The plumb-line represented what God expected of them.

We might say that Malachi's message on faithfulness represents two aspects of God's plumb-line for his people: faithfulness in general and faithfulness in marriage.

Much could be said about the first of these matters, faith-fulness in general, and much needs to be said. We live in a day in which people think nothing at all about not keeping their commitments. It is unspeakably tragic that this treacherous dealing has infected God's people. But no part of God's plumb-line is more necessary for us than faithfulness in marriage. This is not easy. It binds and pinches us. We can ignore it, but it will not go away. Preachers can refuse to preach on God's plumb-line for the home, but that in no way removes it.

There is also comfort on this matter. All of us who are married can avoid the painful, traumatic experience of divorce if we will bring our lives to God's plumb-line for the home. Both husbands and wives must do this. We must remember all the factors that make our lives in the home of strategic impor-tance, and we must especially remember that essential ele-ment of taking heed to our own spirits. If we will do these things, we can go far beyond merely avoiding divorce to con-structing homes that will be miniature models of what Christi-anity is all about.

29.
Zacharias: the tragedy of unbelief

Luke 1:5-25

Here we have a very wonderful message and a most lamentable tragedy. Zacharias was a priest, but he was much more than that. It is possible to be a religious professional and have no genuine regard for God and his laws, but Zacharias and his wife were 'righteous before God, walking in all the commandments and ordinances of the Lord blameless' (Luke 1:6). Zacharias and Elizabeth were godly people. The loved, served and obeyed God, and they believed that God was going to fulfil his promise of the coming Messiah.

All would seem to be well here. Where is the tragedy? It unfolded on one of the days that Zacharias was responsible for serving in the temple. His duties that day required him to burn incense (v. 9). This was a daily ritual in which the priest went very near the veil that separated the Holy Place from the Most Holy Place. Zacharias was to place the incense on the burning coals on the altar. This would cause a cloud of fragrance to arise. It represented the thanksgiving of God's people for the redemption that they enjoyed through the shedding of blood.

The people were outside waiting for Zacharias to return from the altar of incense. They waited and waited, but he did not appear. What had happened?

Luke tells us an angel of the Lord appeared to Zacharias while he was in the Holy Place (v. 11). That angel later identified himself as Gabriel (v. 19).

The message from Gabriel

Gabriel had a message for Zacharias on this day. This was a special message, a delightfully wonderful and glorious message consisting of two parts. First, Gabriel shared this announcement with Zacharias: 'Do not be afraid, Zacharias, for your prayer is heard; and your wife Elizabeth will bear you a son, and you shall call his name John' (v. 13). Then Gabriel proceeded to assure Zacharias that his son would be no ordinary son but would in fact be the forerunner of the Messiah himself (v. 17).

The response of Zacharias

Such good news calls for tremendous rejoicing, but Zacharias was not filled with joy. He responded to this good news by asking, 'How shall I know this? For I am an old man, and my wife is well advanced in years' (v. 18).

There is only one sight that is almost as tragic as that of the unbelieving unbeliever and that is the unbelieving believer. Here we have the sad spectacle of Zacharias in the role of the unbelieving believer. He was a believer in God and his promises, but he did not believe the word from God that Gabriel had just delivered to him.

Reasons for belief

It is indeed a very sad spectacle. Zacharias had every reason to believe. The fact that an angel stood right there before him should have been enough to convince him that the message was bound to come true. On top of that, he and Elizabeth had been praying for the first thing Gabriel announced, a son, and, as people of faith, had been hoping for the second thing, the coming of the Messiah. Here, then, is the shocking sight of a man praying and hoping for things he never expected to receive.

Furthermore, Zacharias had historical precedent to guide and encourage him at the very point that troubled him. The Old Testament, which he loved and revered, told him that his whole nation of Israel came about as the result of an old couple having a son. Abraham's body was 'as good as dead' (Heb. 11:12), and his wife Sarah was well beyond the ability to conceive. But that did not stop the Lord. He and a couple of his angels dropped by one day to assure Abraham and Sarah that nothing was too hard for the Lord and that they would indeed have a son (Gen. 18:1-15). Zacharias knew all about this, and he still refused to believe. He allowed what he knew about his circumstances to override what he knew about God.

We cannot read the response of Zacharias to Gabriel's message without comparing it with what we find later in this same chapter. In the sixth month of Elizabeth's pregnancy (yes, God's word did come true), Gabriel appeared to the Virgin Mary to announce that she had been chosen to bear the Messiah (Luke 1:26-38).

Gabriel's message to Mary placed her in a situation that was both like and unlike the one in which Zacharias found himself. The situations were alike in this way: each heard a message that seemed incapable of fulfilment. While Zacharias was asked to believe that he and Elizabeth would have a son in their old age, Mary was asked to believe that she would bear a son without a human father (vv. 34-35).

Their situations were different, however, in that Mary did not have as much evidence for believing as Zacharias did. While Zacharias could look to the Old Testament and find the account of Abraham and Sarah, there was no such account for

Mary to read. No virgin had ever conceived and given birth to
a child.

Mary differed from Zacharias at another point as well. After
she heard Gabriel's message, she quietly responded, 'Behold
the maidservant of the Lord! Let it be to me according to your
word' (v. 38).

The results of Zacharias' unbelief

But let's return to Zacharias. Gabriel did not take his response
of unbelief lightly. Upon hearing it he declared: 'I am Gabriel,
who stands in the presence of God, and was sent to speak to
you and bring you these glad tidings. But behold, you will be
mute and not able to speak until the day these things take
place, because you did not believe my words which will be
fulfilled in their own time' (vv. 19-20).

So the last thing Zacharias said for nine months was a word
of unbelief. When he was at last able to speak again, he broke
into the torrent of praise that should have been on his lips
when Gabriel first appeared (vv. 67-79).

Examples of unbelieving believers

Thomas

The sad reality of unbelieving believers is mentioned again
and again in Scripture. Thomas refused to believe that Jesus
had risen from the grave although the other disciples were
giddy with excitement over having seen him. Their joy could
not dispel the sombre cloud of gloom that hovered over him.
'Unless I see in his hands the print of the nails, and put my
finger into the print of the nails, and put my hand into his
side,' he solemnly intoned, 'I will not believe' (John 20:25).

Thomas already had, mind you, sufficient evidence for believing that Jesus had indeed risen from the grave. He had heard
the predictions of Jesus to that effect (Matt. 16:21; 17:22-23;
20:17-19). Just a few days before Thomas made his dark vow,
he had seen Jesus step up to the tomb of Lazarus and raise him
from the dead (John 11). Even before this, Jesus had raised
two others from the dead (Mark 5:35-43; Luke 7:11-15) and
Thomas, as one of the twelve who accompanied the Lord
throughout his ministry, would certainly have known about
these events, even if he did not witness all of them with his
own eyes. But all of this was not enough for him.

The disciples on the road to Emmaus

Then there were the two men who, on the day of Jesus' resurrection, were travelling from Jerusalem to Emmaus. Like
Thomas, they had more than sufficient reason for believing
that the resurrection accounts they had heard were true, but
they refused to believe until the risen Lord himself walked
with them in the way, rebuked their slowness to believe and
'expounded to them in all the Scriptures the things concerning
himself' (Luke 24:25-27).

The continuing danger of unbelief

It would be wonderful if the tragedy of unbelieving believers
were relegated to the pages of Scripture but, sadly enough, it
is still very much with us today. We do not, as Zacharias did,
receive the word of God from the angel Gabriel but, make no
mistake about it, we have received the Word of God. We have
in Scripture the revealed truth of God. And we have, even as
Zacharias did, abundant reasons for believing that Word of
God. The fulfilled prophecies of Scripture are sufficient in and

of themselves to convince us of the complete reliability and trustworthiness of the Bible, and there are many more evidences to go along with them.

The similarities between Zacharias and our own situation go still further. The sure and reliable truth of God that we have in Scripture confronts us with the same option that confronted Zacharias. We can either believe or refuse to believe. Indications are that many Christians are just as reluctant to believe the Word of God in Scripture as Zacharias was to believe it from the mouth of Gabriel. It is not that we totally disbelieve the Bible. It is rather a matter of degree. We do not believe it to the extent that we ought. We subscribe generally to its teaching, but we want to reserve the prerogative to trim a little here and to hedge a little there. We want to be selective believers, believing those parts of Scripture that we like, while refusing to believe the parts that go against our personal preferences and popular opinion.

Zacharias speaks to us from the distant past about this matter. He urges us from the pages of Scripture to believe God fully, even when it seems to be foolish to do so.

Our happiness and joy as believers are in direct proportion to the measure of our faith in the Word of God. If we have great faith, we shall have great blessedness. If we have little faith, we shall have diminished blessedness. Let us, therefore, be great believers.

30.
Martha: the trap of jumbled priorities

Luke 10:38-42

Let's make one thing clear right from the start. Martha was not wrong to be concerned about preparing food for Jesus and his disciples. It is certainly legitimate when we have guests in our home to be concerned about their comfort and to provide for their needs.

But yet Jesus rebuked Martha. It was a gentle rebuke, to be sure. We can almost hear Jesus saying, 'Martha, Martha,' and we realize this is no stern denunciation, but rather a tender rebuke that flowed from genuine concern for Martha herself.

Gentle as it was, it was still a rebuke. And we find ourselves wondering why, if Martha was engaged in something that was legitimate, the rebuke was necessary.

Some try to get around the problem by taking the words 'One thing is needed,' to mean that Martha should have prepared only one dish instead of several. But it is obvious from the words that followed that the contrast is not between one dish and several, but rather between what Martha chose, serving in the kitchen, and what Mary chose, listening to Jesus (Luke 10:42). So we are back to the question: why would Jesus rebuke Martha for doing something that was proper and legitimate?

We can only understand why Martha was wrong when we place her actions alongside those of Mary. When Jesus began to speak — and the implication is that he began to teach his disciples — Mary began to listen, while Martha continued bustling about with her preparations. Everything had to be just right, and the more Martha worked to make it so, the more agitated she became. Finally, she reached breaking-point, marched into the presence of Jesus and demanded that he rebuke Mary for leaving her. By the way, the fact that Mary had 'left' Martha indicates that she had been helping but had stopped assisting when Jesus began teaching. In all likelihood more than enough food had already been prepared before Jesus ever arrived (he did, after all, have a habit of giving people advance notice of his visits — Luke 9:52; 10:1; 22:8).

But Martha could not leave it there. She had to go on and on and on with the preparations until she was exhausted — and angry! So the spirit in which Martha was going about her work was quite as wrong the work itself.

When, then, do legitimate things become wrong? When we put them above spiritual concerns! By continuing to give herself to her work, when the Word of God was being taught, Martha fell into the trap of jumbled priorities. She allowed her concern for the good to crowd out the best. She allowed the constant, mundane part of life to eat up what was unique, tremendously significant and swiftly passing — that is, the opportunity to hear Jesus teach. Jesus had come to provide her with a spiritual feast, but she could not receive it because of her preoccupation with her own feast, a feast of temporal things. She was guilty, therefore, of carrying a legitimate concern to an excessive level, and, in doing so, had failed to take advantage of that which was truly crucial.

If we have a tendency to take Martha's side on this occasion, it could very well be because we all too easily see ourselves in her. If we wince at Jesus' rebuke of her, it could very well be because we know that we deserve it ourselves. The truth is that we all have a tendency to engage in Martha's way of living. We are faced time after time with something that is truly crucial and something that is passing and ephemeral, and time after time we choose the trivial and carry it to excessive levels.

Much of our happiness in this life rests in avoiding the trap of jumbled priorities, in learning what really counts and living accordingly. It sounds easy, but most of us are finding it to be anything but. We may rest assured that the Spirit of God saw to it that this account was given to us so that we might slip the shackles of living in Martha's way. And we can slip them by keeping in mind three enormously significant principles.

The priority of the Lord

First, the Lord is always to be our priority over everything else. The Lord Jesus allows us no quarter here. When a scribe approached Jesus to ask which is the greatest commandment of all, the Lord Jesus replied in no uncertain terms: ' "You shall love the Lord your God with all your heart, with all your soul, and with all your mind." This is the first and great commandment' (Matt. 22:37-38).

Does not your own heart tell you that this is indeed life's supreme priority? Think about it. Your very life is a gift from God. Your health, your family, your friends, your skills, your possessions — all are a gift from almighty God. As James tells us, 'Every good gift and every perfect gift is from above, and comes down from the Father of lights...' (James 1:17).

In addition to all of these things, the Christian readily confesses that the same God has bestowed upon him the greatest of all gifts, the gift of forgiveness of his sins and, on that basis, this same God will eventually bring him safely into realms of eternal glory.

In the light of all these things, is it not reasonable to say that the Lord should be our priority? How few professing Christians actually give him that place! How all of us need to hear the rebuke of the Lord: 'But why do you call me "Lord, Lord," and not do the things which I say?' (Luke 6:46).

The importance of the Word of God

Giving priority to the Lord leads, in turn, to a second principle: we cannot give the Lord priority without giving his Word priority.

The Lord Jesus does not leave it to us to define for ourselves how we should go about this business of giving him priority. He affirms again and again that it is a matter of consistently taking in his words and governing our lives accordingly.

Jesus maintained that his words were so important and vital that a person's whole life could be defined in terms of them. His teaching on this point is exceedingly clear. On one occasion, he insisted that the hearing and heeding of his words enables one to be a wise builder who is able to construct a life that is strong and sturdy. Refusing to hear and heed his words makes another person a foolish builder who is not able to construct such a life (Matt. 7:24-27; Luke 6:47-49).

He affirmed the priority of his words on another occasion in which another woman had fallen into the trap of jumbled priorities. This woman cried to Jesus from the crowd: 'Blessed is the womb that bore you, and the breasts which nursed you!' Jesus responded by saying, 'More than that, blessed are those who hear the word of God and keep it!' (Luke 11:27-28).

When we come to this matter of hearing and heeding the Word of our Lord, we are dealing with a matter that is at the very core of the life of the church. Her worship services are designed to set the Word of God before us. And here is where the account of Martha really hits home. When we have the opportunity to hear the precious word of our Lord, what do we do with it? If we place the fleeting, trivial concerns of this life — no matter how legitimate they may be in and of themselves — above the hearing of the Word of God, we might as well call ourselves 'Martha!'

It does not matter whether it comes in the shape of a baseball, basketball, football or in the form of picnics, fishing tackle, films, concerts, or television shows — when we put it ahead of the Word of God, we have joined Martha in the kitchen.

What, child of God, is the name of your kitchen — that thing, legitimate in its own way, that you use to excuse yourself from hearing and heeding the Word of God?

The lasting good

There is yet another principle suggested by this episode from days gone by, a principle which may be put in this way: giving priority to the Word of God produces good that can never be taken away.

We must never forget that the Lord Jesus was not concerned just to rebuke Martha but also to commend Mary. In doing the latter, he explicitly said Mary had chosen the 'good part', and he would not take it away from her (Luke 10:42).

A passage of Scripture often contains more than one level of truth. It was certainly so when Caiaphas said it was necessary for Jesus to die so that the whole nation might not perish. He was speaking about the raw political necessity of getting Jesus out of the way but, unwittingly, he also proclaimed the central truth of the gospel — that it was necessary for Jesus to die so that others would not perish (John 11:49-52).

I suggest we can treat the words of Jesus about Mary in the same way. On the surface level, they simply mean Jesus was refusing to honour Martha's demand. He would not deprive Mary of the privilege of hearing his words by sending her back to the kitchen. But we do no violence to Scripture if we take those words as a picture of an even greater truth: the words of Christ do good that can never be taken away from those who heed them.

There is, of course, a great day of 'taking away' for all of us. Practically all the things we hold near and dear in this life are going to finally be taken away from us. Martha's kitchen is going to be closed down. All those things that we have used to excuse ourselves from the Word of God will finally perish, but that very Word that we so often avoided will be left. The prophet Isaiah says, 'The grass withers, the flower fades, but the word of our God stands for ever' (Isa. 40:8).

And on that eternal day those who have paid much heed to the Word of God will be shown to be wise, and those who have not sufficiently heeded it will feel ever so foolish for putting the fleeting, trivial things of this life above that blessed Word. May God help us to live now as we shall wish that we had lived on that day.

31.
Simon Peter: the temptation to deny Christ

John 18:15-18,25-27

We come in this chapter to what is certainly one of the saddest episodes in the Bible. Given the opportunity to stand up and speak up for Christ, Simon Peter failed. He failed, not once, not twice, but three times.

There was so much Simon could have said about the Lord Jesus Christ. He was there when Jesus turned water into wine (John 2:1-11). He was there when Jesus healed his mother-in-law of a high fever (Luke 4:38-39). Simon Peter had seen Jesus feed five thousand with five barley loaves and two small fish (John 6:1-13). He was there when Jesus walked on the stormy sea (John 6:15-21). He was there on the Mount of Transfiguration when Jesus glowed with heavenly glory (Luke 9:27-36). Peter had seen Jesus heal the lame (John 5:1-9) and the blind (John 9:1-7). He had even seen Jesus raise three people from the dead (Mark 5:37-42; Luke 7:11-15; John 11:43-44), one of whom had been dead four days (John 11:39).

In addition to all these things, Simon Peter had, by his own admission, heard in the words of Jesus the authentic ring of the message of eternal life (John 6:68).

Simon Peter could have talked about all these things and many, many more. He could have responded to the enquiry of the servant girl and those with her by affirming that he was a disciple of Jesus Christ and that he was glad to be among that number. He could have said that knowing Jesus was the supreme treasure of his life, that no matter how many days he had remaining, he knew of a certainty that nothing else would approach the inestimable privilege that he had in those days in which he walked with the Lord Jesus.

The shameful denials

Yes, that is what he could have said, but he did not. He had the opportunity to stand firm for Christ and bear witness, but he faltered and failed. He had the opportunity to be a solid rock but, in the words of Kent Hughes, he proved to be 'a cracked rock'.[1]

How shameful were Peter's three denials! He did not even attempt to soften them. He could have said, 'You have confused me with someone else,' or 'I don't know what you are talking about.' But he spat his denials out in the most unambiguous and emphatic way imaginable: 'I am not!' (John 18:17,25). Matthew tells us that Peter went so far as to lace his denials with cursing (Matt. 26:74).

The reason for denial

Why did Simon Peter do it? Why did he deny the very one to whom he owed so much? Why did he refuse to confess his allegiance to the one who had rescued him from sin and so often thrilled him with joy unspeakable and full of glory? Biblical commentators have ranged over a good bit of ground in seeking to explain the reason for Simon's denials. Some point out that he had been very proud and self-confident earlier that night (Mark 14:29-31), and that pride always precedes a fall. Some suggest that it was all due to the fact that he had been

sleeping when he should have been praying (Mark 14:37-38).
Some observe that he had set himself up for failure by warm-
ing himself at the fire of those who obviously were not friends
of Jesus (Mark 14:67; Luke 22:55). Some affirm that all of
these considerations must be taken into account in any explanation for Peter's denials.

Peter's fear

While we may see some legitimacy in all of these, they do
seem to miss the most obvious thing — that is, Peter's fear.
He was afraid of what might happen to him if he professed
allegiance to Jesus. By this time Jesus' predictions of his death
(Matt. 16:21; 17:22-23; 20:17-19) must have finally begun to
sink in. Peter now realized at last that Jesus was certainly going to die, and he was afraid that if he admitted to being his
disciple, he too would die along with his Master. The looming
spectre of dying alongside Jesus drove Peter right away from
confessing Jesus.

Our fears and denials

All of this hits painfully close to home. Every Christian knows
what it is to be afraid of what will happen if we let our allegiance to Christ be known — afraid of what others will think
or say about us, afraid that we shall be thought to be unsoph-
isticated, narrow, biased and benighted, afraid that we might
be deprived of that job or that promotion we hope for, afraid
that we shall be considered to be out of step. So it is very easy
to pretend, either that we have no allegiance to Christ at all, or
that we have not allowed any allegiance we may have to take
us to extremes.

There are many ways of hiding or misrepresenting that allegiance. It can be something as simple as not wanting someone

to see that we have a Bible in our possession. It can be a matter of using profanity and by so doing essentially saying, 'I don't want anyone to know that I belong to Christ, so I will talk as if I don't.' It can be a matter of maintaining silence when our Lord is attacked and vilified — that is, acting as if we approve of what is being said.

Every Lord's Day the children of God are faced with this blunt question: 'Will I let my allegiance to Christ be known today by going to public worship?' Or, to put it another way, every Lord's Day we are confronted with this question: 'Am I going to let other interests and allegiances (such as athletic events and family activities) take priority over my allegiance to Christ and his church?'

Sometimes the temptation to deny Christ comes in the form of denying his teachings. For instance, we are commanded to forgive those who trespass against us (Matt. 6:12; 18:21-22). If we refuse to do so, we deny our Lord.

In this area of our Lord's teachings, we must also note that we deny him when we feel compelled to remove or downplay those truths that we consider to be offensive to those around us. Someone may, for example, find it very attractive to say to those around him, 'Yes, I am a Christian, but I don't believe in all that stuff about judgement and hell.'

These and similar situations are not easy for us, but we can stand for Christ in them. We do not have to fail as Peter did. Queen Esther in the Old Testament faced a situation much like the one in which Simon Peter found himself, but she did not fail.

An example of boldness

Because of his bitterness against a Jew, Mordecai, the prime minister of Persia, Haman, had hoodwinked the king into issuing a decree that all the Jews be executed (Esth. 3:1-15). Little did he know that Esther herself was a Jew (Esth. 2:20).

This situation demanded that Esther go before the king and intercede for her people, but there was a serious problem. Anyone who came into the king's presence without being summoned by him would be put to death unless the king extended his sceptre (Esth. 4:11), and Esther had not been summoned for a period of thirty days. But Esther, believing she had been brought to the kingdom for that very hour (Esth. 4:14), summoned courage and went to the king on behalf of her people. Confronted with the opportunity to deny her connection with her people, she boldly confessed it. How refreshingly different from Simon Peter!

The bitter consequences

All of us who know the Lord have denied him in one way or another, but no true Christian will ever be comfortable denying Christ. The Gospel accounts tell us that Peter's denials caused him to weep bitterly (Mark 14:72; Luke 22:62). No Christian will regard his denials of Christ as light and trivial matters. They will weigh heavily upon him and bring grief to his heart until he finds a place of repentance. Even after repentance, the memory of those denials will cause him shame. If, on the other hand, there is no sorrow over denying Christ and no repentance of it, it may indicate that we have no Christ to deny but have deceived ourselves about belonging to him.

The matchless grace of Christ

We surely cannot consider Peter's denials of Christ without turning our thoughts to the final chapter of John's Gospel. Simon Peter and some of the other disciples of Jesus had gone fishing in Galilee. These men were probably at a loose end. Jesus had risen from the dead and appeared to them, but they were uncertain as to what the future held for them. Simon Peter may very well have been convinced that whatever Jesus had in mind for the other disciples, it certainly would not include him. If so, he was in for quite a surprise.

As a long, fruitless night of fishing gave way to the dawn, he and those with him could discern a figure in the early morning mist, but they did not know it was Jesus. His command to them to cast their net on the other side of the boat and the subsequent catch were designed to remind them of his early call to them (Luke 5:1-7) and to assure them that this call had not been revoked.

Upon seeing the catch, the men realized the figure on the shore was none other than Jesus, and the impulsive Simon scrambled out of the boat and made his way to him. There on the shore Simon found Jesus had built a fire (John 21:9), and there the Lord Jesus asked him three times whether he, Simon, loved him. It was around a fire that Peter had three times denied Christ, and now around the fire he was given the opportunity three times to confess his love for Christ (John 21:15-17).

In this way the Lord Jesus showed Simon Peter something of the greatness of his grace. It is truly grace that is greater than all our sins, and it will never, no never, let us go. It not only pursued Simon, but also restored him to usefulness and fruitfulness in the work of Christ's kingdom.

I am certainly not glad that Peter denied Christ, but since it is a fact that he did, I am glad that the Gospel writers relate it. I am glad because I can read their accounts and be reminded of the terrible power of sin in the life of the child of God and the glorious reality of the grace of God that forgives, cleanses and restores to usefulness. Even when we are faithless, he remains faithful (2 Tim. 2:13).

32.
Paul and Peter: the peril of compromise

Galatians 2:11-16

Here we have one of the most fascinating of all Scriptures and one of the deadliest of all perils.

This is a fascinating passage because it brings before us a clash between the two leading apostles of the church, Paul and Peter. It is fascinating because it was Paul who confronted Peter.

Peter was one of Jesus' original disciples. He had accompanied Jesus all through his public ministry. He was there when Jesus performed his miracles. He was there on the mountain when Jesus took on a heavenly appearance so that his face shone like the sun and his clothes were white and glistening (Matt. 17:1-2; Mark 9:2-3; Luke 9:28-29). He was there when Jesus demonstrated his power over death by calling Lazarus from the grave (John 11:43-44). He was one of the first to arrive at the empty tomb that had held the body of the Lord Jesus and to see the risen Lord (John 20:1-10; Luke 24:34; 1 Cor. 15:5). He was not only present when the Holy Spirit descended on the Day of Pentecost but also delivered a powerful gospel message on that same day (Acts 2:14-39).

Paul, on the other hand, was a late-comer to Christianity. He had been converted in spectacular fashion when the risen Lord intercepted him on the Damascus Road (Acts 9:1-9). Prior to that he had been the leading persecutor of Christians.

Because of their respective circumstances, Peter enjoyed a priority and dignity that Paul did not have, but this did not deter Paul from confronting and rebuking Peter publicly at Antioch.

What if the current crop of Christians had been the public that witnessed this confrontation? What would have been the prevailing sentiment? Some would say that Paul was wrong, that he had no right to do this, that he was putting doctrine above the unity of the church. Perhaps someone would have offered this assessment: 'Paul had better learn his place. He has no right to rebuke someone of the stature of Peter.' And perhaps someone would add: 'And Peter is such a nice fellow.'

Unity, dignity, being a 'nice' person — these and similar considerations have been escorted inside today's church and seated at the head of the table while doctrine is left outside begging in the streets.

Why is this the case? The church has reached the melancholy conclusion that doctrine is just not all that important, that a person can believe whatever he or she likes and it will not finally matter. On top of that, doctrine is considered to be divisive, and those who emphasize it are counted as difficult, narrow and contentious people who enjoy a good theological brawl.

Such doctrinal squeamishness would have astonished Paul, especially on the point of doctrine that was at issue in Antioch. It was not a fine, obscure point that brought him to his feet and into conflict with his fellow apostle. It was the very essence of the gospel itself. How important is doctrine? It can be this important: eternal destiny hangs upon a true understanding of Christianity's central doctrine of salvation through Christ and Christ alone.

Peter's compromise

This was the situation in Antioch. When Peter first arrived there, he had no scruples at all about sitting down to eat with Gentile and Jewish Christians. He treated them equally. We are not surprised at this. Peter had been taught by the Lord by means of a vision that there are no second-class citizens in the kingdom of God (Acts 10:9-16).

Then one day the beautiful harmony at Antioch was shattered. A party of Christians from Jerusalem stopped by. These people apparently claimed to represent James, the half-brother of Jesus and the leader of the Jerusalem church (Gal. 2:12). Paul says that they were 'of the circumcision' (v. 12). In other words, this party consisted of Jews from Jerusalem who believed that faith in Christ alone was not a sufficient basis for fellowship between Jews and Gentiles.

When this group arrived, Peter changed. He had been eating with the Gentile Christians, but the old nemesis that had driven him to deny his Lord, fear of man, once again raised its ugly head.

Glyn Owen takes us to the heart of Peter's action in these words: 'Of course, Peter's change of stance did not mean that he ceased to believe that a repentant sinner is saved by faith alone in Christ alone. But it did mean that he now *acted as if* he no longer believed like that. The whole thrust of the passage is that he became hypocritical in his behaviour: he *acted as if* he believed that a circumcised man had something to commend him, that an uncircumcised man had not; he *acted as if* he believed that the circumcised constituted an élite group in the church, whereas the uncircumcised were second-grade believers with whom one could not have fellowship. And in acting as if he believed these false ideas, which detracted from both the glory and the sufficiency of the Lord Jesus Christ, the great apostle Peter, even at this advanced stage of his life and career, behaved in such a way as to cast a cloud over the gospel'[1] (italics are his).

Paul's correction

It was too much for Paul. He saw the danger inherent in Peter's action. No sooner had Peter withdrawn from the Gentile Christians than Barnabas, who had stood with Paul on this very matter in the past (vv. 1,9), followed Peter's example and withdrew from the Gentiles. Paul could see, then, the spectre of a divided church, one section Jewish, the other Gentile, looming before him.

But it was his zeal for the gospel itself that propelled Paul into action. Paul says Peter and Barnabas were not being 'straightforward about the truth of the gospel' (v. 14). They were not walking on the straight path of the gospel but were deviating and straying from it.

Some would have us believe that the gospel is an ambiguous, nebulous thing that can never be accurately defined, that it can mean one thing to one and something quite different to another. But Paul would have none of this. The gospel is a clearly defined path, and it is the responsibility of all Christians to walk straight down that path.

What is the gospel? Paul himself gives us a wonderfully concise statement of it in these words: ' ... a man is not justified by the works of the law but by faith in Jesus Christ ... that we might be justified by faith in Christ and not by the works of the law; for by the works of the law no flesh shall be justified' (v. 16).

John R. W. Stott says the gospel 'is the good news that we sinners, guilty and under the judgement of God, may be pardoned and accepted by his sheer grace, his free and unmerited favour, on the ground of his Son's death and not for any works or merits of our own'.[2] 'More briefly,' Stott writes, 'the truth of the gospel is the doctrine of justification (which means acceptance before God) by grace alone through faith alone...'[3]

By withdrawing from the Gentile Christians, Peter was essentially denying the truth of the gospel. He was imposing upon the Gentile Christians a condition for fellowshipping with them, circumcision, which God had not imposed upon them in justifying them.

Peter's response

To Peter's credit, he accepted the rebuke of Paul and began again reflecting the truth of the gospel in his behaviour. How do we know this to be true? Soon after Paul had rebuked him, Peter stood up at the Council of Jerusalem and spoke these words: 'Men and brethren, you know that a good while ago God chose among us, that by my mouth the Gentiles should hear the word of the gospel and believe. So God, who knows the heart, acknowledged them by giving them the Holy Spirit, just as he did to us, and made no distinction between us and them, purifying their hearts by faith. Now therefore, why do you test God by putting a yoke on the neck of the disciples which neither our fathers nor we were able to bear? But we believe that through the grace of the Lord Jesus Christ we shall be saved in the same manner as they' (Acts 15:7-11).

Peter, publicly confronted by Paul for compromising the truth of the gospel, publicly stood for that truth at this council. Still later, he referred to Paul as 'our beloved brother' (2 Peter 3:15). It is obvious that Peter accepted the rebuke without despising the one who administered it.

A question

I find it quite impossible to read the account of Paul's confrontation with Peter without asking this question: 'What if Paul were alive today?' It is a searching question. What would Paul say if he could sit in our churches? What would he say if he could rub shoulders with us for a while? Would he be pleased to find us steadfastly adhering to the purity of the gospel? Or would he find it necessary to confront us openly as he did Peter at Antioch?

Such questions probably seem to be ridiculous to many. Most evangelicals feel that their gospel house is in good order. If there is any area in which we believe ourselves to be on solid ground, it is on this matter of fidelity to the gospel. Is it possible that we are not as solid as we think?

The temptations to compromise the gospel are numerous and subtle. We compromise the gospel when we succumb to the pluralistic spirit of our world and move the gospel from the only way to one way among many.

Salvation by being a 'nice' person is a widely held view in our world; in other words, nice people automatically go to heaven. Salvation by death is another widely held view; that is, all one has to do to go to heaven is simply die. To whatever extent evangelicals are influenced by such views, or lulled into condoning them, they compromise the gospel.

Sometimes the compromise comes, not from actually embracing these erroneous views, but rather from allowing ourselves to be so intimidated by them that we mute some of the essential doctrines of the gospel. If we soft-pedal the radical sinfulness of man, the unyielding holiness of God and the certainty of coming judgement, we compromise the gospel.

If we weaken or soften the gospel demands, we are also guilty of compromise. How easy it is us for us to turn the gospel demand for sincere and deep repentance of sin and conscious submission to the authority of Christ into 'accepting' Christ or 'inviting' him into our lives by smilingly and breezily walking down an aisle and saying a prayer. It should not surprise us that so many of our 'converts' have no interest in living according to the commands of one before whom they have never truly submitted as their sovereign Lord. We should not expect them to be willing to do in their 'Christian' walk what they were not willing to do when they made their profession.

These are gospel-huckstering days in which pastors and churches look upon the gospel as their 'product' that they are free to adjust and massage to meet the changing whims and the felt needs of the hearers. But the gospel is not, and never has been, man's product. It is God's divine revelation. And his call to the church today is to refrain from tampering with it and give herself to faithfully proclaiming and living it. Only as we do so do we avoid the peril of compromise.

33.
Onesiphorus: resisting the temptation of the easy option

2 Timothy 1:13-18

Three of the apostle Paul's letters are known as the 'Pastoral Epistles' because they deal with the duties of those who are called to lead local churches.

Two of these letters went to Timothy and one to Titus. Timothy was raised in a godly home (2 Tim. 1:5; 3:15), and came to know the Lord through Paul's ministry (1 Tim. 1:2). When Paul was in Lystra, he added Timothy to his missionary team. Later he sent him to pastor the church in Ephesus.

Timothy was still in Ephesus when Paul wrote the two epistles addressed to him, and he was caught in a devastating crossfire. On one hand, the times were extremely difficult and not at all hospitable towards the gospel (2 Tim. 3:1-9). On the other hand, he was facing challenging problems in the church. Such things would have been frightening enough for the strongest of men, but Timothy was anything but strong. In addition to being prone to a fearful timidity (2 Tim. 1:6-8), he suffered from physical problems (1 Tim. 5:23). Things had become so bad in Ephesus that Timothy had evidently asked Paul to give him a new assignment.

Paul could have sternly rebuked Timothy for being so weak and for wanting to find a way out of his assignment, but he did not. Instead he offered Timothy an impressive array of comforts and encouragements. Among other things, Paul reminded

Timothy of the faithfulness of the Lord Jesus Christ to his task (1 Tim. 6:13), of the faithfulness of his grandmother and mother (2 Tim. 1:5) and of the glory of salvation (2 Tim. 1:8-12).

And in an almost subtle manner, Paul reminded Timothy of Onesiphorus. Here is a man we all need to meet and remember. He was an example to Timothy of how to serve the Lord, and he is an example to all of us who know the Lord. We have encountered many who stumbled in their service to the Lord because they did not withstand the various perils and temptations associated with Christian service. This man Onesiphorus comes as a welcome relief. Here is a man who did not stumble in his service because of a peril. Here is a man who overcame the temptation to take the easy way out but rather gave himself diligently to serving.

Service undetermined by others

The first thing we can say about Onesiphorus' service to the Lord is that it was not determined by the performance of others.

It should not escape our notice that Paul mentions two other men before he mentions Onesiphorus. We know very little about these two men, Phygellus and Hermogenes. They are mentioned nowhere else in Scripture. Paul mentions these two men in connection with those in Asia who had 'turned away' from him (v.15). Evidently they were the ringleaders in this turning away.

Some commentators think it was Paul's arrest in Asia that precipitated this turning away. His arrest may have made it seem that the whole Christian cause was lost. Or it may have made it seem as if Christianity was just too costly. Whatever the cause of it, this turning away was widespread. But it did not touch Onesiphorus. While others were turning away, he remained steadfast. While others were ashamed of the chains of Christianity's leading spokesman, Onesiphorus was not. The tide in Asia was going against Paul, but that did not bother Onesiphorus. If the tide was going against the way he wanted to go, he would just go against the tide.

We have here, then, two models of Christian service. On one hand is the Phygellus-Hermogenes model. It says, 'Serve the Lord when it is convenient and popular to do so.' On the other hand is the Onesiphorus model that just says, 'Serve the Lord! Serve him when it is popular and when it is not. Serve him when it is convenient and when it is not. Serve the Lord!'

Which model do you follow? There are many indications that the Phygellus-Hermogenes model is much in vogue today. Church membership rolls are swelled with people who served for a while but then gave up. Perhaps they started in a time when their church was filled with excitement. But now the excitement has waned and so has their commitment. The Lord has not changed. His promises have not changed. The spiritual needs of those in the community have not gone away. The glory of redemption has not changed. But these people have changed. They have taken their cue from Phygellus and Hermogenes. The followers of Phygellus and Hermogenes are numerous today. Thank God, we can still find men and women like Onesiphorus.

The needs of others

A second thing we must notice about Onesiphorus' service is that it was directed towards the needs of others.

It is obvious from these verses that Paul considers what Onesiphorus did to be service to the Lord. He speaks of the reward that Onesiphorus can expect to receive from the Lord (2 Tim. 1:18). But as we read these verses, we see that Onesiphorus was serving the imprisoned Paul. We might, therefore, be inclined to ask, 'Which was it? Was Onesiphorus serving Paul, or serving the Lord?' And the answer is: 'Both!' Here is a very important and vital connection: we serve the Lord when we serve others. Onesiphorus made this connection. We often do not.

In these days in which Christians equate serving the Lord with enjoying a spiritual 'high' in church, we would do well to think of those around us who are in need of ministry, as Onesiphorus did.

Impressive as the example of Onesiphorus is, we can look to one who is even greater: the Lord Jesus himself. During his earthly ministry, Jesus said to his disciples, 'And whoever of you desires to be first shall be slave of all. For even the Son of Man did not come to be served, but to serve, and to give his life a ransom for many' (Mark 10:44-45).

In his letter to the Philippians, the apostle Paul focused on the example of Christ: 'Let each of you look out not only for his own interests, but also for the interests of others. Let this mind be in you which was also in Christ Jesus, who, being in the form of God, did not consider it robbery to be equal with God, but made himself of no reputation, taking the form of a bondservant, and coming in the likeness of men' (Phil. 2:4-5).

Diligent and persistent

A third thing for us to notice about the service of Onesiphorus is that it was diligent and persistent. Paul makes mention of the fact that while he was in Ephesus, Onesiphorus had ministered to him in 'many ways' (2 Tim. 1:18).

For a man to minister in many ways in his own setting would seem to be sufficient, but it was not for Onesiphorus. When he learned that Paul was imprisoned in Rome, Onesiphorus made his way there and ministered to him. He could have stayed in

Ephesus saying, 'I have done enough for Paul, much more than others.' But the spirit of service so gripped his heart that it propelled him to Rome.

Once in Rome he was faced with a very large obstacle. Paul was imprisoned there, but where? There was almost certainly no central registry of all prisoners that Onesiphorus could check. The only thing left for him was to go from dungeon to dungeon looking for Paul. So from dungeon to dungeon he went. He did not stop with the first or second or third, but kept going until he found Paul. The apostle's grateful astonishment for the diligence and persistence of this man is conveyed by these words: 'He sought me out very zealously and found me' (v.17).

Those words thrill my heart, not only because of what they tell us about the Christian service of Onesiphorus, but also because of the hint they give of the redeeming work of Christ. I can, along with every other Christian, say the same thing of the Lord that Paul said of Onesiphorus: 'He sought me out very zealously and found me.' Thank God!

Our Christian service, so often haphazard and easily forsaken, could certainly profit from a strong dose of diligence and persistence such as Onesiphorus possessed. He shows us that we are to work hard and keep doing so in our service to the Lord.

A heart touched by the graciousness of Christ

One more thing must be said about the service of Onesiphorus: it flowed from a heart that had been touched by the graciousness of Christ.

Every Christian has been touched by the graciousness of Christ, but some Christians reflect that graciousness with which they have been kissed to a higher degree than others.

Onesiphorus possessed and reflected it to a very high degree. The apostle Paul says, 'He often refreshed me' (v.16).

Onesiphorus was one of those rare gems in whom the warmth and love of Christ so flourished that he was a joy to be around. To appreciate this, all we have to do is think of the reverse of it. We all know miserable Christians whose presence drains and taxes us, people who go to minister to others and always end up droning on and on about themselves and their own problems. Let us learn from them and yearn to be like Onesiphorus.

I can visualize Timothy reading of the refreshing spirit of Onesiphorus and going back to his work with renewed vigour. Let us read of Onesiphorus and do the same.

34.
The church of Ephesus: the danger of love growing cold

Revelation 2:1-7

The second and third chapters of Revelation contain letters from Christ to seven of his churches. These letters were recorded by the apostle John, but they are from the risen Lord. They reflect, not John's assessment of these seven churches, but Christ's.

In the very first of these letters, the Lord Jesus Christ reminds the Ephesians that he is indeed perfectly qualified to evaluate them. He identifies himself as the one who holds the seven stars in his right hand and who walks in the midst of the seven golden lampstands (Rev. 2:1).

We know that the lampstands represented the churches themselves and that the stars represented the 'angels' of those churches (Rev. 1:20). Various proposals have been made regarding the identity of these angels. Perhaps the most widely accepted view is that they are the pastors of those churches.

The fact that Christ holds these seven stars in his right hand indicates that he not only gives them to the churches but also directs and protects them. Every pastor who understands these stars to represent himself finds a wealth of consolation in so doing. True pastors are in the hands of Christ, given to the church by the Lord and directed and protected by the Lord.

The fact that Christ stands in the midst of the seven lampstands not only indicates that he continually observes his churches, but also that their purpose is to cast light on him. How many churches are failing in their God-ordained responsibility to shine on Christ so that he may be made visible to an unbelieving world? How many churches are guilty of obscuring Christ rather than shining on him?

Having identified himself to his church in Ephesus, the Lord Jesus proceeds to offer his people there a commendation, a rebuke, an exhortation and an encouragement.

Christ's commendation (vv. 2-3,6)

There was much to commend in the church of Ephesus. This church was energetic and persistent in service, passionate about holiness and sound in doctrine.

Energetic and persistent in service

The Lord noted the 'works' and the 'labour' of the Ephesians (v. 2). These people were not merely sitting on their hands. They were actively engaged in serving the Lord. And they did not go about this service in fits and starts. They persevered in it without becoming weary (v. 3). In this time in which it is very difficult for most churches to find energetic, steady workers, we certainly must admire the way the church of Ephesus went about serving the Lord.

Passionate about holiness

We must also admire their passion for holiness. The Lord notes that they could not 'bear' evil people (v. 2). A few verses later he commends them for hating the deeds of the Nicolaitans (v. 6). This sect may very well have sprung from the Nicolas who was set apart as a deacon by the early church (Acts 6:5).

This man evidently championed the view that a person could be a Christian and live as licentiously and promiscuously as he desired. Clement of Alexander says of those who followed him: 'They abandoned themselves to pleasures like goats, leading a life of self-indulgence.'[1]

The Ephesians were to be commended because they understood that a commitment to Christ is a commitment to holiness, and they refused to cave in to the Nicolaitan view.

The Nicolaitans have not died. They live in everyone who espouses the 'carnal Christian' view that maintains that it is possible to be saved and yet live continually in sin.

Sound in doctrine

The Ephesians' resistance to the Nicolaitans is evidence enough that that they were sound in doctrine, but the Lord also commended them for testing those who professed to be apostles and finding them to be liars (Rev. 2:2).

All of those who find themselves inclined to decry or play down the importance of doctrine would do well to reflect long and hard on the simple fact that the risen Lord commended the Ephesians for their embrace of sound doctrine.

Christ's rebuke (v. 4)

With so much to commend in this church of Ephesus, we might be inclined to think that the Lord would have no word of rebuke to offer, but he did. And a stern rebuke it was. He says, 'Nevertheless I have this against you, that you have left your first love.'

As pleased as the Lord is, then, with energetic, persistent service, passion for holiness and soundness in doctrine, he desires more. He wants his people to love him with a fervent love.

Every Christian loves Christ. One cannot be a Christian without loving Christ. But there are degrees of love. Sometimes the flame of love burns brightly, while at other times it barely flickers and appears to be on the verge of being extinguished.

The Christian's first love is fervent love. When he comes to know Christ, he is amazed at what has happened. He was a guilty sinner who deserved nothing but God's eternal condemnation. But through Christ he has been forgiven and cleansed and made part of the family of God, and all of these incredible blessings have come to him from the grace of God. He has done nothing to earn or deserve them. He has been made a citizen of heaven apart from any merit of his own.

If someone should come along and ask the new convert if he loves Christ, he would receive an immediate and emphatic 'Yes!' The pressing question for the new convert is not whether he loves Christ, but rather how to express that love. He is anxious to do whatever he can to show his love for Christ, and he cannot conceive of being asked to do something for Christ that he would not be willing to do.

Every Christian begins with this fervent love, but, alas, we do not stay there. Satan has a vested interest in chilling the love of God's people (cold hearts pose no threat to him), and he has all sorts of devices to accomplish this chilling. Perhaps it is the siren sound of the world and the lusts of the flesh. Perhaps it is discouragement or disappointment in the work of the Lord. Perhaps it is the hardship of various trials and afflictions. Or it may be the combined weight of all of these that causes our hearts to drift away from the Lord and our first love to become a distant memory.

Christ's exhortation (v. 5)

The Lord did not take the cold hearts of the Ephesians lightly. He said, 'Remember therefore from where you have fallen; repent and do the first works, or else I will come to you quickly and remove your lampstand from its place — unless you repent.' Repentance is the central thing in those words. To repent is to acknowledge from the heart the reality and depth of our sins and to turn with sorrow and resolution from them.

It is true, of course, that Christ also called upon them to remember their first love and do the first works, but these are what we might call the 'book-ends' of repentance. One book-end is *remembrance*. Before repentance can be genuine, there must be deep and thorough reflection on the spiritual vibrancy that was once ours. This is the fuel for repentance. If we do not believe we have lost anything we will not be driven to repent.

The other book-end is *performance*. They were to do again the first works. The Bible knows nothing of a repentance that does not lead to change in conduct. The Ephesians were to demonstrate the reality and genuineness of their repentance by actually returning to conduct that manifested hearts aflame with love for Christ.

They could not afford to be half-hearted and nonchalant about Christ's call to repentance. How often God's people are! We hear calls to repentance without realizing how very important and vital such calls are. To help his people in Ephesus understand the imperative nature of his call to repentance, the Lord added a warning about what would happen if they refused. Their lampstand would be removed. They would cease to be a church.

Christ's encouragement (v. 7)

The Lord Jesus could have ended his letter on that sombre note, but instead he chose to add this sparkling word of encouragement: 'To him who overcomes I will give to eat from the tree of life, which is in the midst of the Paradise of God.'

Our hearts and our lives are barometers of our spiritual condition. A heart that is so cold that it refuses to repent finally gives evidence that it has not been regenerated by grace. The regenerated heart knows what it is to fluctuate and vacillate in love for Christ, but it will persist in doing so until the believer is finally brought into that glorious setting in which the fluctuations and vacillations will all be over, and he or she will for ever be lost in wonder, love and praise.

Section V
Grace greater than the perils we face

This is a book about perils, or dangers, because we live in a dangerous world. The greatest of all the dangers we face in this life are spiritual in nature. No one is free from them. Satan places various temptations and hindrances in the way of unbelievers to keep them from coming to faith in Christ. But even believers are not free from dangers. Satan throws all kinds of obstacles in their way to thwart them from faithful service to the Lord.

We might find that the mere study of the dangers we face leads only to yet another peril, the temptation to discouragement and despair. When the apostle Paul thought about the nature of the gospel ministry he cried out, 'Who is sufficient for these things?' (2 Cor. 2:16). A serious look at the perils and dangers all around us could very well cause that same question to arise in our minds. Indeed, who is sufficient for such things?

Paul answered his question by saying, 'Our sufficiency is from God' (2 Cor. 3:5), and that must be our answer for facing the spiritual perils that confront us. We are not sufficient for them, but God's grace is sufficient for us.

35.
Grace sufficient to overcome the dangers

Grace is a many-splendoured thing. It has more dazzling facets to it than the most brilliant diamond. A brief look at just three of these facets will be more than enough to cheer and steady us in the face of the most fearsome array of snares and dangers that Satan can muster against us.

Saving grace

It is God's grace that saves, and no matter how many hurdles and obstacles Satan places in the way of the sinner, God's grace is sufficient to overcome them.

Electing grace

No sinner is saved by accident. All who are saved must finally attribute their salvation to God's plan to save them, and God made this plan before the world began. This brings us to the great mystery of God's election. No word is more disconcerting and dismaying to unbelievers. It affirms that there is absolutely nothing in this business of eternal salvation that we can take credit for, that it is all of God. It is so completely and

entirely his work that he in eternity past made for all Christians
the decision he knew they could never make, and would never
make.

We shall never be able to understand the doctrine of election apart from the reality and depth of human sin. And to
understand sin we must go back to the very beginning of history. The book of Genesis tells us that our father Adam disobeyed God, and in so doing brought the dreadful calamity of
spiritual death upon himself and all his descendants.

Perhaps the most crucial question any of us can ever ask is
this: how far did Adam fall? How we answer that question
will determine what we believe about salvation.

There can be no doubt about how the apostle Paul answered
this question. He asserted that Adam's fall was total; in other
words, no part of him was left untouched by his sin, and because he was the representative head of all of us, we have to
say we are just as much affected by sin as he was. Adam's sin
left his mind so darkened that he could no longer comprehend
the truth of God, and that darkness of mind is ours as well
(1 Cor. 2:14; 2 Cor. 4:4). Furthermore, Adam's sin left his heart
so degraded that he began to set his affections on earthly things
rather than on God, and those degraded affections are ours as
well. We are constantly gripped by the lust of the flesh, the
lust of the eyes and the pride of life (1 John 2:16). Finally,
Adam's sin even touched his will. His will, once alive to God
and eager to embrace God's will, was deadened by his sin.
That same deadness of will affects all of us so that we do not
naturally desire God or seek after him (Rom. 3:10-11). Sin
has so blasted our minds, affections and wills that it makes no
more sense to talk about man searching for or choosing God
than it does to talk about a mouse searching for or choosing a
cat.

But God in astonishing grace did not leave us entirely to
ourselves. He could have done so, but he did not. He would

have been completely just and fair if he had merely left us to the consequences of our sins. But in grace he determined to take out of the sinful human race a people to redeem, to sanctify and finally to glorify. And he determined to do all this before the world began.

The apostle Paul plainly states this doctrine in the ninth chapter of his letter to the Romans. There he reminds his readers of what God had taught Moses: 'I will have mercy on whomever I will have mercy, and I will have compassion on whomever I will have compassion' (Rom. 9:15). From those words Paul draws this conclusion: 'So then it is not of him who wills, nor of him who runs, but of God who shows mercy' (Rom. 9:16).

Salvation is completely a matter of the grace of God. Before the world began he chose his people (Eph. 1:4). His reason for doing so was entirely 'the good pleasure' of his will (Eph. 1:9). In making his gracious choice, God in no way showed injustice or unfairness. He would have been totally just if he had not extended his grace to any. He would have been wonderfully gracious if he had extended it to only a few. But the truth is that God has chosen a vast multitude to share in his eternal glory (Rev. 5:9-10).

Some have taken such passages to mean that God did nothing more than look down the corridor of time, see those who would choose him and then choose them first. But this argument cannot stand up to careful scrutiny. In the course of his defence of the doctrine of election, Paul warns about the tendency to 'reply against God' (Rom. 9:20). Now if the doctrine of election amounted to nothing more than God choosing those whom he knew in advance would choose him, there would be no one objecting and replying against God. The replying against God comes when people find that they can contribute absolutely nothing at all to their salvation but are shut up completely unto the grace of God.

In addition to these things, we must also note that the fact that God made this choice does not mean he is in any way arbitrary or capricious. R. C. Sproul explains in this way: 'An arbitrary choice is one made for no reason at all. Though Reformed theology insists that God's election is based on nothing foreseen in the individuals' lives, this does not mean that he makes the choice for no reason at all. It simply means that the reason is not something God finds in us. In his inscrutable, mysterious will, God chooses for reasons known only to himself. He chooses according to his own pleasure, which is his divine right. His pleasure is described as his *good* pleasure. If something pleases God, it must be good. There is no evil pleasure in God'[1] (italics are his).

All of this should cause all of us who know the Lord to stand in awe and adoring worship before him. Of course, it is a great mystery. We shall never plumb the depths of it in this life, but the fact that we cannot understand it does not make it false.

Calling grace

What encouragement is there for us in this matter of God's electing grace? The Lord Jesus answered this question by saying, 'All that the Father gives me will come to me, and the one who comes to me I will by no means cast out' (John 6:37).

The apostle Paul stated the same truth in these words: 'Moreover whom he predestined, these he also called...' (Rom. 8:30).

Let the devil rage and churn out a thousand malicious machinations and schemes. His contrivings will not keep even one of God's elect from coming to true faith. Those whom the Father has planned to save will be operated on by the Holy Spirit of God. They will be given life by the Spirit and made to see their sinful condition and the righteous judgement of God coming towards them. They will also be enabled to see that

Christ, and Christ alone, is their only hope of being able to stand clean and uncondemned before a holy God and, once they see that, they will repent of their sins and entrust themselves wholly to Christ. All of this is made clear to them primarily through the preaching of the gospel of Jesus Christ (Rom. 1:16-17; 10:14; James 1:18; 1 Peter 1:22-23).

What Paul said of the Christians in Thessalonica can, then, be equally well said of each and every child of God: '... God from the beginning chose you for salvation through sanctification by the Spirit and belief in the truth, to which he called you by our gospel...' (2 Thess. 2:13-14). Those whom God chose invariably and infallibly come under the influence of the Spirit of God and are called by him through the preaching of the gospel to believe the truth of the gospel.

Keeping grace

Testimonies from the apostle Paul

Another glorious aspect of the grace of God is this: all those who are chosen by God and called by the Spirit are also kept or preserved. This is part of the golden chain of redemption. As it is sure that the chosen will be called, so it is sure that the called will be glorified. This is clear in the words that we just noted from Paul to the Thessalonians. After mentioning the choosing and the calling of the Thessalonians, he adds this phrase: 'for the obtaining of the glory of our Lord Jesus Christ' (2 Thess. 2:14).

Paul adds this same link to the chain in his much-loved eighth chapter of Romans. We have already noted how he links there the choosing (or predestining) and the calling. But he does not stop there. He also says, 'These he also glorified' (Rom. 8:30).

A testimony from the apostle Peter

A further indication of this truth is found in the First Epistle of Peter. After addressing his readers in terms of the grace of God that had worked, and continued to work, in their lives, the apostle describes the inheritance God's people will receive in heaven. He characterizes this inheritance in three ways: it is incorruptible, undefiled and unfading (1 Peter 1:4). It is not capable of decay. It cannot be tainted by sin. And it is beyond the reach of change.

Peter also says this inheritance is being kept for us by God. He says it is 'reserved' in heaven (1 Peter 1:4). It is, in the words of John Gill, 'out of the reach of men and devils'.[2]

Last of all, Peter declares that we are being kept for this inheritance. He says his readers are 'kept by the power of God through faith for salvation ready to be revealed in the last time' (1 Peter 1:5). It is being kept for us and we are being kept for it. And the one who is doing the keeping is the sovereign, omnipotent God. This inheritance is one that is really secure!

While we rejoice in the cheering truth that God keeps his own, we must make sure we do not distort it. Peter does not say that God keeps all those who profess to know Christ, no matter how they live. This has in fact been what many have said. The 'carnal Christian' teaching maintains that it is possible for a person to be saved and yet go on living as if he were an unbeliever. But Peter makes it plain that God keeps his people in a certain way — that is, 'through faith'. Christians do have their lapses, but that is different from continually living in sin and apart from God. The general tenor of the Christian's life is continuing in the faith. This is how God keeps him.

A testimony from the book of Revelation

Revelation 17:14 also gives us a glimpse of God's keeping grace. There we find Christ sharing his victory over Satan and his forces with 'those who … are called, chosen, and faithful'. It is very important that we pay attention to those words. Christ's victory is shared by those who are called and chosen, and these are the same ones who are faithful to him. Michael Horton is correct when he writes, 'That they remain faithful is as much a gift of God's grace as their election and calling.'[3]

It is not hard to see what God's keeping grace has to do with the dangers that Christians face. Even when we miserably fail and fall into one of the snares and temptations that surround our path, we can never thwart God's purpose of grace in our lives. We are in the hand of God (John 10:28-29) and nothing can break that mighty grip.

> I grasp thy strength, make it mine own,
> My heart with peace is blest;
> I lose my hold, and then comes down
> Darkness, and cold unrest.
> Let me no more my comfort draw
> From my frail hold of thee;
> In this alone rejoice with awe —
> Thy mighty grasp of me.
>
> (John Campbell Shairp)

We can, therefore, rejoice in these oft-quoted lines from Augustus M. Toplady:

> The work which his goodness began
> The arm of his strength will complete;
> His promise is Yea and Amen,
> And never was forfeited yet;
> Things future, nor things that are now,
> Not all things below nor above
> Can make him his purpose forgo,
> Or sever my soul from his love.

My name from the palms of his hands
Eternity will not erase;
Impressed on his heart it remains
In marks of indelible grace;
Yes, I to the end shall endure,
As sure as the earnest is given;
More happy, but not more secure,
The glorified spirits in heaven!

Restoring grace

Yet another aspect of God's marvellous grace has particular relevance for this matter of the child of God facing various dangers. In addition to keeping us, God's grace also restores us. Keeping grace means our sin can never sever our relationship with God. Restoring grace means we can be restored to fellowship with God and usefulness in his kingdom even after we have grievously sinned. Keeping grace assures that the Christian will never become an apostate. Restoring grace assures that the backsliding Christian will find forgiveness with the Lord.

We have already encountered this grace in preceding chapters. Simon Peter experienced restoring grace. The Christ whom he had denied would not let him go but rather pursued and restored him (John 21).

King David experienced it in the Old Testament. God's restoring grace enabled him to see the horror of his adulterous affair with Bathsheba and his subsequent arrangement to have her husband killed. That grace led him to honestly and candidly identify his actions by their right names ('transgressions,' 'iniquity,' 'sin' and 'evil'), and to cry for God's mercy and cleansing (Ps. 51:1-4). It caused him to see that his sin constituted an assault upon God himself and to join with God in condemnation of his sin (Ps. 51:4). It further led him to pray: 'Restore to me the joy of your salvation, and uphold me by your generous Spirit' (Ps. 51:12).

In Psalm 32 David rejoices in the restoring grace of God. There he writes:

> I acknowledged my sin to you,
> And my iniquity I have not hidden.
> I said, 'I will confess my transgressions to the Lord,'
> And you forgave the iniquity of my sin
>
> (Ps. 32:5).

While the children of God can never lose their salvation, they can and do backslide. They know what it is to stray from their Lord and into sin. They can, like those we have noted in previous chapters, find themselves in the clutches of various perils. They can be guilty of unfaithfulness and compromise. They can deny their Lord and grow cold in their love for him. They can be seduced by their culture and even fall into the clutches of unbelief. But the same grace of God that saved them will not let them go. It will make them miserable in their sins and will ultimately bring them to repentance. How thankful we should be for God's stubborn grace!

The channel of God's grace

We must not rejoice in the many marvels of God's grace without reminding ourselves of how it comes to us. The emphatic answer of Scripture to that query is the Lord Jesus Christ. He, and he alone, is the channel through which the saving, keeping and restoring grace of God flows to us.

There is a terrible tendency these days to separate the grace of God from the Lord Jesus Christ, to suggest that we can receive the benefits of God's grace apart from the work of Christ. Those who fall into this error do so because they separate God's grace from his justice. Those who imagine that God's justice can be safely ignored, that it constitutes no threat, will never adequately prize the work of the Lord Jesus Christ.

God's grace can never flow to us until the demands of his justice are satisfied, and here is why the work of the Lord Jesus is so absolutely indispensable: he satisfied on behalf of his people the demands of God's justice. He became their surety. He came to this world with their human nature, adding it to his own divine nature, and in that human nature did all for them that God's justice required. On their behalf he lived in perfect obedience to the demands of God's law, and on their behalf he on the cross received the penalty of God's wrath. Those for whom he died deserved that penalty because of their sins but Christ, their surety, paid it in their stead.

Because of the work of Christ there is not one demand of God's justice that has been left unsatisfied. There is not one debt outstanding. All has been paid by Christ. And with the demands of God's justice satisfied, there is now no impediment to the free flow of God's grace.

Because of Christ we need not fear Satan and the various temptations and threats he churns out. Christ is sufficient for all. He is sufficient to save us from our sins and to keep us and to restore us even when we fail.

Jesus! what a friend for sinners!
Jesus! love of my soul;
Friends may fail me, foes assail me,
He, my Saviour, makes me whole.

Jesus! what a strength in weakness!
Let me hide myself in him;
Tempted, tried, and sometimes failing,
He, my strength, my vict'ry wins.

Jesus! what a help in sorrow!
While the billows o'er me roll,
Even when my heart is breaking,
He, my comfort, helps my soul.

Jesus! what a guide and keeper!
While the tempest still is high,
Storms about me, night o'ertakes me,
He, my pilot, hears my cry.

Jesus! I do now receive him,
More than all in him I find,
He hath granted me forgiveness,
I am his, and he is mine.

Hallelujah! what a Saviour!
Hallelujah! what a friend!
Saving, helping, keeping, loving,
He is with me to the end.

(J. Wilbur Chapman)

Notes

Chapter 1 — Cain: a warning against self-centred living
1. Michael Scott Horton, *Made in America: The Shaping of Modern American Evangelicalism*, Baker Book House, pp.78-80.
2. S. G. DeGraaf, *Promise and Deliverance*, vol. i, Paideia Press, p.51.

Chapter 2 — Esau: a warning against living for the present
1. Quoted by Warren W. Wiersbe, *Treasury of the World's Great Sermons*, Kregel Publications, p.40.

Chapter 3 — The Philistines: a warning against fighting God
1. Josh McDowell, *Evidence that Demands a Verdict*, Campus Crusade for Christ, Inc., p.23.
2. As above.
3. Arnold Dallimore, *George Whitefield: The Life and Times of the Great Evangelist of the Eighteenth-Century Revival*, Cornerstone Books, vol. i, p.31.
4. McDowell, *Evidence that Demands a Verdict*, p.23.

Chapter 4 — Jeroboam: an example of falling into the 'convenience' trap
1. George Barna, *What Americans Believe*, Regal Books, p.29.

Chapter 5 — Jeroboam: trying to divide or hide from God
1. Matthew Henry, *Matthew Henry's Commentary*, Fleming H. Revell Publishing Company, vol. ii, p.651.

Chapter 8 — Three men: three hindrances to following Christ
1. Leon Morris, *The Gospel According to St. Luke*, Wm B. Eerdmans Publishing Co., p.180.

Chapter 13 — Judas Iscariot: a warning against apostasy
1. S. G. DeGraaf, *Promise and Deliverance*, Presbyterian and Reformed Publishing Co., vol. iii, pp.152-3.
2. Samuel E. Waldron, *A Modern Exposition of the 1689 Confession of Faith*, Evangelical Press, p.222.

Chapter 15 — Naaman: overcoming the temptation to stand on our dignity
1. Maclaren, Alexander, *Expositions of Holy Scripture*, Baker Book House, vol. ii, p.361.

Chapter 16 — Nathanael: overcoming prejudices against the truth
1. Leon Morris, *The Gospel According to John*, Wm. B. Eerdmans Publishing Co., p.171.

Chapter 17 — Saul of Tarsus: overcoming scepticism
1. Alexander Maclaren, *Expositions of Holy Scripture*, Baker Book House, vol. xi, p.265.

Chapter 18 — The people of Israel: a warning against idolatry
1. Michael Horton, *In the Face of God*, Word Publishing, p.21.

Chapter 19 — Achan: the danger of selfish individualism
1. Barna, *What Americans Believe*, p.300.

Chapter 20 — Samson: the perils of a seductive culture
1. Sproul, R. C., 'Table Talk,' July 1991, p.31.
2. Jordan, James B., *Judges: God's War Against Humanism*, Geneva Ministries, 1985, p.272.

Chapter 21 — David: living under the burden of guilt
1. Joel Gregory, *Growing Pains of the Soul*, Word Books, p.43.

Chapter 24 — The man of God from Judah: subjective experience and the Word of God
1. John MacArthur, *The Charismatics*, Zondervan Publishing House, p.59.

Chapter 25 — Hezekiah: dealing with moral filth
1. Henry, *Commentary*, vol. ii, p.997.
2. As above.

Chapter 27 — Jonah: a warning against running from God
1. O. Palmer Robertson, *Jonah: A Study in Compassion*, The Banner of Truth Trust, p.15.
2. As above, p.16.

Chapter 28 — Malachi: a warning against unfaithfulness
1. T. Miles Bennett, *The Broadman Bible Commentary: Malachi*, Broadman Press, vol. vii, p.368.
2. Joyce G. Baldwin, *Haggai, Zechariah, Malachi*, Inter-Varsity Press, pp.240-41.

Chapter 31 — Simon Peter: the temptation to deny Christ
1. Kent Hughes, *Mark: Jesus, Servant and Savior*, Crossway Books, vol. ii, p.183.

Chapter 32 — Paul and Peter: the peril of compromise
1. J. Glyn Owen, *From Simon to Peter,* Evangelical Press, p.364.
2. John R. W. Stott, *Only One Way: The Message of Galatians,* Inter-Varsity Press, p.54.
3. As above.

Chapter 34 — The church of Ephesus: the danger of love growing cold
1. John MacArthur, *The MacArthur Study Bible,* Word Bibles, p.1994.

Chapter 35 — Grace sufficient to overcome the dangers
1. R. C. Sproul, *Grace Unknown,* Baker Books, p.147.
2. John Gill, *Exposition of Old & New Testaments,* The Baptist Standard Bearer, vol. ix, p.531.
3. Michael Horton, *Putting Amazing Back into Grace,* Baker Books, p.213.